INCREDIBLE VOLLEYBALL

Wally Dyba

York University

Good Luck with your coaching.
Wally Dyba

Sport Books Publisher

Graphics and design by Takao Tsuruoka and My1 Designs

Library and Archives Canada Cataloguing in Publication

Dyba, Wally, 1949-
    Incredible volleyball lead-up games and drills / Wally Dyba.

ISBN 0-920905-74-9

1. Volleyball – Training. I. Title.

GV1015.3.D92 2005   796.325   C2004-904068-5

Copyright © 2005, by Sport Books Publisher
All rights reserved. Except for use in review,
no portion of this book may be reproduced or
transmitted in any form or by any means without
Written permission of the publisher.

Copyeditor: Patricia MacDonald
Proofreader: Patricia MacDonald

Photo credits: Paul Constantinou, Sport York at York University

Distribution worldwide by
Sport Books Publisher
278 Robert Street
Toronto, ON M5S 2K8
Canada

http://www.sportbookspub.com
E-mail: sbp@sportbookspub.com
Fax: 416-966-9022

Printed in Canada

ACKNOWLEDGEMENTS

First and foremost, I would like to thank Dr. Peter Klavora for encouraging me to take on this project. He believed in this book from the beginning. His enthusiasm and patience during the years of writing are greatly appreciated.

I cannot fully express my gratitude to Peter Maione. His subtle humour, tireless intensity, and superb guidance made the task a joyful experience. The numerous meetings were always productive.

I would like to thank Merv Mosher and Hernan Humana, who many consider two of the greatest minds in the sport of volleyball. I am very honoured to be considered a friend and a colleague. I have been fortunate to have had the opportunity over the years to share and discuss thoughts and ideas on how we can more effectively teach the game of volleyball to players and coaches.

My gratitude to the many individuals who were a part of the various camps, clinics, and symposia I participated in. You were the ones who unknowingly provided the feedback when many of the concepts were being tried and tested. The days and nights at Madawaska volleyball camp and the York University volleyball seminars are particularly noted.

I would be remiss not to mention all the students in my practicum classes and the players on the many teams that I have coached over the years – in particular my children Janique and Rob. You were the inspiration to try to make the teaching and practice environments more effective and enjoyable.

And finally, my wife Denise. You have provided the foundation from which I draw my strength.

LEAD-UP GAMES AND DRILLS

CONTENTS

ACKNOWLEDGEMENTS *3*

PART I: EFFECTIVE COACHING METHODS *8*

TASK ANALYSIS *9*

SKILL PRESENTATION TECHNIQUES *10*

UNDERSTANDING THE PLAYER AS AN INFORMATION PROCESSOR *10*

IMPORTANCE OF FEEDBACK IN EFFECTIVE COACHING *12*

LEARNING STAGES *14*

COACHING TACTICS *15*

DEVELOPING COMPETITION SMARTNESS *16*

PLANNING AN ALL-YEAR TRAINING PROGRAM *18*

PART II: MOTIVATION AND INSPIRATION *20*

THE COACH AS A MOTIVATOR *21*

MOTIVATION FOR PRACTICE *22*
  • Useful motivational strategies *22*

FINAL THOUGHT *25*

INSPIRATIONAL SLOGANS *25*

CONTENTS

PART III: HOW TO PLAY THE GAME   34

OBJECTIVES OF THE GAME OF VOLLEYBALL   35

VOLLEYBALL RULE CHANGES AND ADDITIONS   36

BASIC VOLLEYBALL CONCEPTS   38

THE BASIC VOLLEYBALL PLAY (BVP)   40

DEVELOPING AN UNDERSTANDING OF THE BASIC VOLLEYBALL CONCEPTS   42
- The one-on-one situation   43
- The two-on-two situation   46
- The four-on-four situation   48
- The five-on-five situation   54
- The six-on-six situation   58
- Service reception formations   60
- Team play worksheet   73

PART IV: LEAD-UP GAMES   74

DEVELOPING TECHNICAL SKILLS WITHOUT THE BALL   76
- Movement   76
- Agility   78
- Jumping   82

DEVELOPING TECHNICAL SKILLS WITH THE BALL   84
- Getting used to the ball   84
- Serving   86
- Passing and receiving   89
- Attacking   94

DEVELOPING TECHNICAL AND TACTICAL SKILLS WITH AN OPPONENT   98
- Serving and receiving   98
- Complex passing   102
- Attack defence   105

DEVELOPING ADVANCED PLAYING ABILITY   108
- Mini-games   108
- Games with opponents of unequal numbers   112

LEAD-UP GAMES AND DRILLS

PART V: DRILLS 114

CHART 1 – TECHNIQUE AND TACTICS WITHOUT THE BALL 118

POSTURE AND MOVEMENT 119
- Basic volleyball posture 119
- Volley pass posture 120
- Forearm pass posture 120
- Service posture 120
- Block posture 121
- Movement 121
- Posture and movement drills 122

CHART 2 – VOLLEY PASS 130

THE VOLLEY PASS 131
- Technique and control drills – Individual 133
- Using the net as an obstacle 134
- Technique and control drills – Partners 135
- Movement drills – Partners 137
- Group drills 138
- Back volley drills 140
- Application of the volley pass in mini-games 142

CHART 3 – FOREARM PASS 144

THE FOREARM PASS 145
- Technique and control drills – Individual 146
- Using the net as an obstacle 147
- Technique and control drills – Partners 148
- Movement drills – Partners 148
- Group drills 149

DIGGING – BACKCOURT DEFENCE 151
- Drills to develop the skill 151

CHART 4 – SERVE 154

THE SERVE 155
- Drills to develop the skill 157
- Service and service reception 159

CONTENTS

CHART 5 – ATTACK   *162*

THE ATTACK   *163*
- Drills to develop the skill   *164*

CHART 6 – BLOCK   *168*

THE BLOCK   *169*
- Drills to develop the skill   *170*

CHART 7 – SUMMARY OF INDIVIDUAL TECHNIQUE AND TACTICS WITH THE BALL   *171*

CHART 8 – TEAM PLAY   *172*

TEAM PLAY   *173*
- Setting up the drills   *174*
- Drills to develop the skill   *178*

PART VI: CIRCUIT TRAINING   *184*

CIRCUIT 1   *186*

CIRCUIT 2   *188*

CIRCUIT 3   *190*

CIRCUIT 4   *192*

PART VII: GLOSSARY   *194*

PART I

TASK ANALYSIS 9

SKILL PRESENTATION TECHNIQUES 10

UNDERSTANDING THE PLAYER AS AN INFORMATION PROCESSOR 10

IMPORTANCE OF FEEDBACK IN EFFECTIVE COACHING 12

LEARNING STAGES 14

COACHING TACTICS 15

DEVELOPING COMPETITION SMARTNESS 16

PLANNING AN ALL-YEAR TRAINING PROGRAM 18

EFFECTIVE COACHING METHODS

Peter Klavora, University of Toronto

The basic idea of coaching volleyball is the development of players' technical and tactical skills as well as their physical and psychological abilities. As a result, each of these components should be carefully developed during practice. These abilities and skills are initially tested in practice and training games, where conditions can be controlled and monitored, before moving on to more important competitive situations that serve as tests for future performance potential. The goal of practice should be to develop consistent performance during competition, which is vital for success.

There is a growing body of research on a wide range of learning and coaching principles that make coaching volleyball effective. Eight of these concepts, designed to enhance the methodology of coaching volleyball, are presented in this section. They deal with (1) the systematic analysis of the volleyball task; (2) skill presentation techniques; (3) the understanding of the athlete's limitations in processing information; (4) the importance of feedback in effective coaching; (5) the appreciation of the learning stages; (6) coaching tactics; (7) the development of competition smartness; and (8) the need to plan an all-year training program.

Task analysis

Any volleyball skill can be broken down into a set of component movements that are quite distinct from each other in terms of the operations needed to produce an effective performance. The component movements of the task are envisaged as the ***subroutines*** involved in the total performance. Together, the subroutines form the overall task, which is conceived as an ***executive plan***. This executive plan then is the overall goal, aim, or objective the player is trying to master; at the same time it serves as an organizational process that controls the order in which a sequence of simpler tasks or movements is carried out.

Each subroutine can be further broken down into simpler movements, the ***sub-subroutines***. The process of division depends upon the complexity of the task at hand. It stops when all basic movements that make up the task are identified.

It is advantageous, therefore, for the coach to break down each of the volleyball tasks into basic movements, ordered from the simplest to the most complex in a hierarchical fashion. Once these hierarchies are formed, the player can easily be introduced to new material at the level most appropriate given his or her past experience. The drill section of the book displays eight charts that present skill hierarchies for all volleyball tasks. Obviously, the less experienced a player, the lower in the hierarchy he or she should begin. Once the basic movements are mastered, the player can attempt movements at the next level in the task hierarchy structure. This process is continued until the most complex movements of the volleyball task are learned.

When learned, the skills at the bottom of each task hierarchy become mainly automatic and are "run off" without much attention by the player. Once they are mastered, these movements are relegated to the lower centres of the brain and do not overload the player's nervous system. Through practices using numerous lead-up games and drills, the execution of well-learned skills becomes automatic.

Skill presentation techniques

The best way to introduce a new skill is demonstration coupled with an explanation of the skill. If the coach does not possess the skill, it can be demonstrated by an athlete or an assistant coach. Other forms of visual information can be used, such as still pictures of proper actions, film clips or videos of successful performances, etc. The instruction should be kept brief and to the point, emphasizing only one or two key points at a time. Furthermore, the teaching formation must be such that all athletes are in front of the demonstrator and have a good view from the proper angle. Several lead-up games and drills designed to develop the same skill must be selected very carefully to assure the right progression in skill development and to prevent boredom. Furthermore, the selected drills should challenge the skill level of the athletes. If drills are too easy, the players may become bored quickly. Conversely, if the drills are too difficult, the athletes may become frustrated with lack of progress in skill development.

Understanding the player as an information processor

Coaches seldom realize that most coaching principles are based on knowledge of athletes' limitations and capacities in receiving and processing information. After a poor performance many coaches begin a long lecture about which bone does what and what muscles to use and at what particular time in the movement this or that muscle is to be activated. In essence, such coaches are observing and commenting only on the end result – the response or output of a whole series of interior processes that go on while the player is trying to execute the new skill at his or her very best. What are these processes?

Psychomotor processes (Figure 1.1) are part of the player's nervous system and are, in most cases, taken for granted. These mechanisms help the learner to sense, perceive,

COACHING METHODS

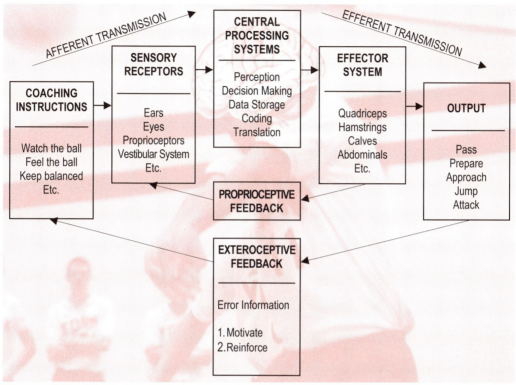

Figure 1.1 Psychomotor processes involved in executing a volleyball skill.

attend to, store or memorize, decide on, and organize an action in relation to the demands placed on him by the coach and the environment. These mechanisms transmit information (***afferent*** and ***efferent*** transmissions) that is flowing between the coach and the athlete. However, these mechanisms are full of limitations that dictate our coaching approaches and teaching strategies. By keeping these limitations in mind, the coach becomes more effective, which in turn helps players to progress faster. Table 1.1 (see page 12) outlines some of the major limitations of athletes' psychomotor systems and the main coaching strategies to overcome these limitations.

It is difficult to separate the player's sensory capacities from his perceptual processes. What input the athlete actually processes is highly dependent upon the quality of her sensory and perceptual mechanisms. In practice, the athlete is constantly bombarded with stimuli coming in through various senses. These stimuli are provided *externally* by the coach (***exteroceptive feedback***) and *internally* by proprioceptors (***proprioceptive feedback***, through receptors in the muscles, tendons, ligaments, and vestibular sense for balance). However, the player's single-channel system or selective attention that serves as a funnel filters out most of the available information presented

Table 1.1 Coaching strategies based on information processing limitations.

MECHANISM	LIMITATION	COACHING STRATEGY
Sensory Mechanisms	• Poor visual skills, such as dynamic visual acuity • Athlete does not hear instructions	• Detect vision problems early • Limit noise in the gym; speak clearly and loudly
Perceptual Mechanisms	• One-track mind; selective attention; can attend to only one major point	• Provide only one critical component of a skill at a time
Short-term Memory	• Limited capacity • Significant rate of loss • Can be easily interfered with	• Provide only a limited amount of information; do not overload athlete • Minimize time between demonstration and rehearsal of skill • Avoid unrelated activities in gym, such as workers in the background, spectators yelling or commenting, other teams practicing, etc.
Long-term or Permanent Memory	• Must rehearse to encode and retain information	• Provide continuing rehearsal of skill until it is learned properly
Player's Psychological State	• Anxiety and arousal • Attention and fatigue • Boredom	• Provide nonthreatening learning environment • Avoid practicing new skills when fatigued • Introduce new drills to coach same skill

to him. If the coach wants the player to perceive (i.e., hear or see) the right things, he would have to select and present instructions carefully so that they have a chance to get through for interpretation and recognition. The single-channel system, selective attention, and short-term memory systems are limitations of the player's perceptual mechanism that every coach must consider for optimal learning results in practice.

Importance of feedback in effective coaching

The coach's instructions, corrections, explanations, interpretations, comments, or notes, directed to the player during practice, evaluate her current performance. This evaluation is the feedback that systematically shapes the player's movements into the desired act, according to the coach's plan. According to motor learning texts, "Practice alone does not make perfect, practice with appropriate feedback makes perfect.... Feedback is probably the single most important factor during practice sessions." This and similar quotations indicate the significance of the presence of meaningful feedback in learning and performance.

The coach's feedback can be either *descriptive* or *prescriptive* in nature. A descriptive feedback statement indicates something about what the player did ("not so good on the follow-through," "try better at next attempt," etc.); it presumes that the player knows what to do on the next attempt. Prescriptive feedback, on the other hand, provides the athlete with information he or she can use to make more effective corrections in the subsequent attempt ("focus on the wrist at the point of contact") at the task. In general, prescriptive feedback is considered more effective than descriptive feedback.

There are five fundamental questions concerning the efficacy of a coach's provision of feedback: (1) when is feedback most beneficial; (2) how much feedback is necessary; (3) how precise should feedback be; (4) what should the timing of feedback be; and (5) motivation properties of feedback.

Stages of learning and feedback The coach's feedback is especially vital early in the learning process. Later in an athlete's training, however, after he has gained experience and developed an internalized model of the correct volleyball skill or task that he uses as a reference pattern, the coach's attention can be reduced and eventually completely withdrawn.

How much feedback is necessary The earlier discussion about the athlete as an information processor should answer the question of how much feedback is necessary for an effective instruction process. Particularly during coaching of novel skills or plays, an athlete's "one-track mind" can process and attend to only a limited amount of information. The athlete can effectively concentrate on only one novel movement. Only later, when she becomes familiar with the novel task, can she shift her attention to other novel tasks and/or share the attention with other requirements of the movement or play. Although the athlete is limited in his capacities to process the coach's information, intense but selective coaching is nevertheless required in the early stages of the player's development if he is to progress at an optimal rate. In other words, no more and no less information about a performance should be provided than the athlete is capable of handling. The instruction must be adjusted to the amount of information the player can use.

How precise should feedback be Motor learning research has suggested that precise coaching generates far better results than any other type. The coach must formulate a precise standard of each task or play he wants to coach. Then, he or she must develop a trained eye in order to be able to provide precise information to the athlete abut his errors and how to correct them.

LEAD-UP GAMES AND DRILLS

To decrease the dependency of athletes on coach's feedback as they become more skilled the coach may consider using *bandwidth* feedback. With this method, the coach only gives feedback when an athlete's movements fall outside some acceptable level of correctness, or bandwidth. This type of feedback has many advantages. The coach gives feedback less frequently and athletes' intrinsic feedback gains in importance, which allows them to strengthen their permanent memory of the skill or play.

Timing of feedback To consider the timing of the coach's feedback to the athlete is to apply his short-term memory limitations to the coaching situation. Short-term memory bank is very susceptible to loss, and generally the greater the delay before giving the athlete information about her performance, the less effect the given information has. Thus, an intense, continuous instruction is more beneficial to the development of skills than the provision of coaching at the end of practice when the team is ready to leave the gym.

Motivation properties of feedback The coach's encouraging words ("good," "excellent," "that's it," etc.) not only provide the athlete with information about her performance but also act as a reinforcement. When the player is given precise information about his technique, this feedback strengthens the correct response. In this regard the coach's instruction increases motivation, and, in general, information about one's performance affects the incentive to do well. It is encouraging for the player to hear that he or she is improving. The improvements make the athlete happy and motivate him to maintain his interest and his desire to keep practicing. Thus, the coach's feedback fulfills a valuable motivational role, as well as shapes and continually reinforces the development of desired skills (see Figure 1.1, page 11).

Learning stages

Technical and tactical training play a central role in developing a complete player. Technical elements of the game are normally developed in three stages of learning: acquisition, stability, and application.

Acquisition stage The goal of this learning stage is to introduce new technical elements to players and have them perform the skills under simplified conditions, initially while standing still, and later with movement. When introducing a skill for the first time, it is important that the coach introduce it in a simplified setting. Initially, rough forms of the skill are developed in relatively undemanding conditions. The player's performance is highly variable and she is generally not aware of exactly what should be done differently the next time to improve. As a result, she needs specific information that will assist her in correcting what she has done wrong. With some practice, the player moves on to the second (stabilization) learning stage.

Stabilization stage The main objective of the stabilization stage is to refine their skills. The errors are fewer and less significant. The players are developing an ability to detect some of their own errors in performing the various tasks and various game elements. This provides the athletes with some specific guidelines about how to continue practice. Variability of performance from one attempt to another also begins to decrease. Gradually, the coach introduces variations according to game demands. Variations can be with regard to movement speed (ball or player), distance, movement direction, etc. Plays should be attempted at a faster tempo, from different distances, from different angles, and, if necessary, from both left and right directions. An important step is to practice game-specific combinations where several game elements are combined into a more demanding practice. Initially, one should choose combination elements that occur immediately before or after the skill just learned. Then, the easiest form should be chosen (depending on the game) and should be practiced in more demanding complex game forms. For example, when practicing attacking, passing the ball prior to the attacking movement can be added.

In order to further strengthen technical abilities, one has to include an opponent, whose impact is guided by the coach. Initially, the skill should be practiced with a passive opponent and with minimal decision-making requirements. Taking an opponent into account, the player has to learn to make simple decisions in order to be successful. The passive opponent eventually becomes a semi-active opponent that agitates the player but still lets him or her successfully complete a rally. The player now has to broaden his or her technical abilities in order to be successful.

The demands get even greater when the opponent becomes an active opponent that not only tries to increase the difficulty of skill execution but also attempts to win the rally. At this point, tactical training becomes important and must be introduced into practice gradually.

Application stage   After much practice and experience with various skills, the athlete moves into the application stage of learning. Here, skills have become almost automatic or habitual. The player does not have to attend to the entire production of the skill, but has learned to perform most of the skill without thinking about it at all.

The application stage is the result of a tremendous amount of practice; it allows players to produce volleyball skills and movements without concentrating on the entire movement. Therefore, they are able to attend to other aspects of the game, such as tactics. The goal of practice becomes learning how to apply the learned technical elements and the game's complex combinations in a game situation within a determined tactical framework. Thus, learning of tactical skills becomes a very important aspect of practice in the application learning stage.

Coaching tactics

The development of tactical abilities is a complicated process because it consists of a multi-layered system of subprocesses that normally develop in three steps:

LEAD-UP GAMES AND DRILLS

Step 1 This step is mainly concerned with strengthening individual and collective tactical methods and variations to solve a specific tactical problem. This includes training of individual movement forms and team combinations with the goal of using them at the right time and place, either alone or with other players. An example of an attack tactic is to "hit the ball by the block." To solve this problem there are several basic forms with variations that can be practiced; initially without an opponent, then with a passive opponent, and then a semi-active opponent. Basic forms include (1) tipping the ball over the block; (2) hitting around the block down the line; (3) hitting around the block cross-court; (4) hitting over the block; (5) hitting off the block; and (6) hitting through the block.

These basic plays and their variations should be introduced one after the other and practiced diligently with the main goal to strengthen their correct execution.

Step 2 The second step involves perceptual and cognitive tasks where the players are learning to correctly assess a game situation and then correctly respond to the specific demands of the game. This requires learning to make quick and good judgements with a semi-active or active opponent.

The player has to learn to recognize a specific game situation, or even create it, in order to use certain tactical elements. For this type of training, lead-up games that closely simulate competition situations can be effectively employed. Various forms of lead-up games are still easier to play compared with scrimmage practice or competition games (fewer players, fewer opponents, smaller court area, etc.).

Step 3 The goal of this step is the correct application of the acquired basic forms and variations in a game. The tasks of this step are to develop the abilities to use tactics in the right situations, and also to develop the ability to create situations where a certain tactic can be used. The latter should be practiced under simpler conditions and in scrimmage practice so that they can be applied appropriately in actual games. In some cases, the practice conditions should be harder than in actual competition.

Developing competition smartness

Training of competition smartness should occupy an important part of a team's practice. It is mainly developed by playing competitive games under four progressively more demanding conditions: (1) simplified conditions; (2) scrimmage practice; (3) more demanding conditions; and (4) competition.

Practice games played under simplified conditions This introductory level of competition is characterized by playing simplified preparatory games using half the court, lower nets, a reduced number of players or an uneven number of players, simplified rules, etc. This results in lower technical requirements. Initially, only simple technical skills are required. With regard to tactics, individual and simple group tactical actions are predominant (Table 1.2).

COACHING METHODS

Table 1.2 Practice games played under simplified conditions.

RULES	TECHNIQUE	TACTICS
• Fewer main rules • Coach-initiated rallies • Altered number of players: ⇒ Fewer players ⇒ One-sided player advantage • Scaled-down equipment: ⇒ Lower net ⇒ Half the court	• Simple technical skills and abilities required	• Easy tactical applications in attack and defence: ⇒ Mainly individual tactical acts ⇒ Simple group tactical acts

Scrimmage practice Scrimmage practice involves practice games within the same team, with the full number of players and regular game rules. From scrimmage to scrimmage, the coach progressively increases the demands by introducing more rules, increasing playing time, and demanding higher intensity of play. Each player should be provided with plenty of opportunities to apply the acquired skills in scrimmage practice. Furthermore, it is important to work on the gradual elimination of technical mistakes.

Another purpose of scrimmage games is to practice the individual and group tactical elements that were practiced in training. In scrimmage practice, the coach is able to interrupt the game and point out mistakes and explain or demonstrate certain aspects or situations. Each player is assigned very specific goals that they are encouraged to apply during practice games.

The constant development and refinement of individual and group tactical elements, as well as the conscious application of these elements during scrimmage practice, lead to a constantly higher quality of play. The coach must ensure that all players have an equal opportunity to play during this stage of development.

Practice games played under more demanding conditions In order to prepare players really well, we recommend practicing games under more demanding conditions. These games provide greater challenge than the standard of competition games. This can be done with regard to physical, tactical, technical, or psychological aspects, but often, the increase of one aspect makes the other aspects harder, too. Table 1.3 (see page 18) shows a few possibilities. When planning games under more demanding conditions, the coach must take into account several factors, such as skill and fitness level of the athletes, the team's tactical abilities, etc. It is important that the players be able to effectively meet more demanding conditions.

LEAD-UP GAMES AND DRILLS

Table 1.3 Practice games played under more demanding conditions.

PHYSICAL ASPECT	TECHNICAL ASPECT	TACTICAL ASPECT	PSYCHOLOGICAL ASPECT
• Extended rally length • Fewer no. of players • Strenuous tactical demands • Carrying weighted vests, etc., during play	• Lower net • Altering no. of players • Playing with weaker hand	• One-sided team superiority • Playing against much stronger opponent • Playing game with four nets • Making higher tactical demands, etc.	• Providing high noise background • Beginning scrimmage at a specific score, e.g., 23–24 • Giving one-sided instructions • Demanding additional training

Competition games played under normal conditions   Successful competition is the goal of all coaching efforts. The players have to demonstrate how successfully they can apply their acquired technical and tactical skills and whether their technical, tactical, physical, and psychological preparation was thorough enough. It is important to find the right tactical concept with its specific variations and to apply it, based on the performance ability of one's own team and of the opponents, as well as their strategy. Competition games should be evaluated thoroughly, and conclusions should be drawn for future training.

Planning an all-year training program

Overall planning of training aims at producing the highest possible individual performance. Since this can be achieved only after many years of preparation, intermediate goals must be set, guaranteeing a systematic buildup of performance. Planning thus comprises long-term development plans and multi-year plans for individual development stages; annual plans; and plans for specific periods and stages within an annual plan, such as preparation for a tournament, tapering for playoffs, etc.

The master plan   To achieve optimal performance in players and the team, an all-year training program must be adopted. Only a carefully planned annual plan over an entire year will assure an optimal development of the athletes' physical and psychological capabilities and skills. No matter what level it is for, an annual plan should contain the following: goals and tasks for each player; performance goals for the team; dates for testing of skills, fitness medical examination, and competitions; specific plans for skill,

COACHING METHODS

Table 1.4 An example of a master plan for an indoor club volleyball season.

DATES	JUN	JUL	AUG	SEP	OCT	NOV	DEC	JAN	FEB	MAR	APR	MAY
PERIOD-IZATION	Transition	Preparation				Competition						
	Transition	General Preparation		Specific Preparation		Pre-Comp		Competition			Taper	Playoff

(NOTE: For more detailed information on periodization, refer to the book *Periodization Theory and Methodology of Training*, by Tudor Bompa. Human Kinetics, 1999)

tactics, and fitness training; and a clear division of the year into subphases.

The master plan must assure a systematic development of training throughout the year until the peak of the competitive season, the playoffs. Detailed division of the plan into shorter periods, also known as *periodization of training*, helps the coach maintain tight control over the continual improvement of the athletes' performance. The various phases in the annual plan, the preparation, competitive, and transitory phases, are determined on the basis of the most important competitions in the season. For most teams, these competitions include respective playoffs (Table 1.4).

The preparation period The main objectives during the preparation period are to create fitness, technical, and tactical prerequisites for further increase in the team's performance during the subsequent competitive period. The preparation period includes a general physical preparation period and a volleyball-specific period. Each period lasts approximately six to eight weeks.

The competitive period The competitive period is divided into pre-competition, main competition, tapering, and playoff competition periods. The principal task of the pre-competition period is to convert all basic capacities of the preparation period into competitive performance. The pre-competition period may include the training camp and exhibition schedules. The main competition period includes the regularly scheduled league games. A short tapering period may be scheduled just before the playoff competition period, the concluding part of the season, begins.

The transition period The transition period commences immediately after the conclusion of the competitive period and may last up to a month. During this period, the players are taking a break from volleyball-related training but should regularly cross-train to maintain a good general fitness level.

PART II

THE COACH AS A MOTIVATOR 21

MOTIVATION FOR PRACTICE 22
    Useful motivational strategies 22

FINAL THOUGHT 25

INSPIRATIONAL SLOGANS 25
    Ability 26
    Attitude 27
    Character 28
    Confidence 29
    Courage 29
    Effort 30
    Leadership 30
    Persistence 31
    Practice 31
    Success 32
    Teamwork 33
    Wisdom 33

MOTIVATION AND INSPIRATION

Peter Klavora, University of Toronto

Motivation in athletes is the key to their effective learning of skills and persistent training at high levels of intensity. It is considered to be the intangible that makes the difference between successful and unsuccessful participation in competition.

One of the most important roles played by the coach is that of motivator. The coach's personality, attitudes and convictions, goals, and motivational strategies are of primary importance to the development of interest, motivation, and attitudes of his players toward training and competition. All of these, in turn, affect the degree of success an athlete will achieve. Therefore, the coach must make an effort to understand the motivational forces that stimulate an individual's athletic participation. The coach must realize that there are different sources of motivation that direct a youngster into the game of volleyball and that later incite her to work long and hard toward achieving success in competition. The coach must accept the fact that his athletes' reasons for participation differ greatly. Therefore, the coach must (1) make an effort to know and understand each player's specific needs, interests, and motives related to participation in volleyball; (2) know the various assessment techniques that will help him identify his athletes' motives; and (3) learn and study the various motivational techniques and strategies designed to motivate players.

The coach as a motivator

The coach's ability to motivate his athletes is essential because, when all factors are fairly equal, teams who succeed are those who are the most highly motivated during practices and those who are also mentally well prepared for competition. When the coach is able to instill a burning desire to succeed in a team, that team will be the hardest-working unit. In other words, if properly motivated, the team will always train hard as long as necessary; this in turn leads to competitive success.

The affection and respect the coach succeeds in generating within the team have always been among the greatest motivators in keeping an athlete working hard in practice. This affection and respect of her athletes must be earned by demonstrating not only a solid technical knowledge but also a number of personal qualities that make the coach effective

LEAD-UP GAMES AND DRILLS

in handling and working with the team. A well-liked coach (1) sets the right mood for practice – this mood is confident and relaxed; (2) is interested in his athletes' overall development and not merely in their athletic achievement; (3) is not an authoritarian nor is he excessively permissive – he sets reasonable rules for practice and is consistent in enforcing them; (4) is a hard worker, is well organized, and tries very hard to make the training environment a pleasant place where athletes usually stay for several hours a day; (5) tries to be supportive and understanding because athletes often arrive at practice tired and weary after a long day of studying and/or work. The coach's smile and concern help the athlete to forget his problems more quickly and to settle into an effective practice.

There is no one way for the coach to earn the aforementioned affections since the personalities of coaches vary. Every effective coach provides leadership that is unique and suited to his personality. However, effective leadership also results from several standardized motivational techniques that can be learned.

Motivation for practice

Every player on the team must develop training discipline and an ability to push herself to the maximum at every practice. These psychological qualities can be acquired only if the player becomes involved in volleyball through a highly motivated program. Such a program makes each athlete approach practice with zest and eagerness and makes each athlete look forward to practice with anticipation. The daily practice becomes an entertaining and satisfying experience that challenges the team intellectually as well as physically. This positive attitude does not happen accidentally; it is the result of a carefully planned motivational program designed by the coach. The program must include several specific, carefully selected procedures that are highly motivational and that incite the team to ever greater training demands. Such a program develops pride in athletes about their acquired skills and physical fitness.

Useful motivational strategies

There are many motivational strategies that have been used effectively in many successful programs. It is not expected that a coach will be able to introduce into his program all of the techniques suggested here, but by incorporating a few into the ones he already practices the coach can expect a positive reaction and a heightened enthusiasm from his players.

Educating the athlete   The contemporary practice on any level of participation taxes the athlete physically and mentally. The athlete who understands the purpose of each phase of his training will give the coach more cooperation and will be more motivated during each practice session than the one who is completely uninformed. Therefore, the coach is wise to take time to explain to the team such concepts as (1) skill biomechanics; (2) the principles of various training methods and the effect on an athlete's physiological adaptation; (3) peaking phenomena; (4) the overload principles of training, etc.

The education of players can be done at regular team meetings. These meetings should be very carefully planned. Such matters as the progress of the team, training plans for the next phase, and the review of the videotapes should also be discussed. Athletes' concerns could also be aired at such meetings in order that the athletes be involved in the program intellectually as well as physically.

The education of athletes should be an ongoing process, before, during, and after practices, when the coach reviews the purpose of these practices and justifies her daily coaching methods. A brief comment or statement, hardly longer than a sentence, often does the job.

Variety in training   Contemporary training is a demanding activity, requiring many hours of work from the athletes. The volume and intensity of training are continually increasing, and the players repeat drills and technical elements numerous times. This, unfortunately, may lead to monotony and boredom, which negatively affect a team's motivation. Therefore, the coach, utilizing a knowledge of a large repertoire of drills, needs to be creative in order to develop skills and movements of similar technical patterns. The coach's capacity to create, to be inventive, and to work with imagination is an important advantage for successful variety in training. Only the coach's imagination limits the variety of activity that can be introduced into daily training. However, it is important that the designed training program follow some general principles that guarantee the necessary short- and long-range goals.

Self-planned workouts   One aspect of successful coaching is to develop self-reliance in athletes. To develop this quality and to further motivate practice sessions the coach may, on a given day every week, let a team member plan all or part of the workout for the team within certain guidelines. The "self-planned workouts" procedure adds to the variety in training and reinforces the education of athletes. This certainly increases motivation for practice because athletes perceive that they are responsible for their own actions as they become more involved.

Rewards as motivators   The coach can set up a reward system that provides symbols of recognition for a practice well done. The system can provide great incentive in practice for most players, since athletes generally demonstrate a considerable need for recognition. The rewards for special achievements can be simple. The coach may award special hats or shirts to the most improved player of the week; or each week the coach may let the athlete who worked the hardest wear a specially coloured shirt; or the player who scores the winning point in a scrimmage receives a pound of jelly beans. Again, the only limitation in setting a successful reward system is a coach's imagination.

It is amazing how much motivation within the team this kind of costless reward system generates. It adds a great deal to the quality of practice as most players try very hard to earn at least one such award here and there. It is important, however, that the reward system be set up in such a way that even the less gifted players can experience some measure of success. It boosts their spirits enormously and lets them know that they too are important and necessary members of the team.

Performance evaluation   Regular performance evaluation throughout the year keeps most athletes enthusiastic and motivated for daily practice at the desired intensity levels. The performance evaluation provides the athlete with the necessary feedback about her own progress from test to test and from year to year. Continuous progress is one of the strongest motivators to an athlete. Achieving short- and long-term goals gives her a tremendous sense of accomplishment, which drives her even harder in practice.

Performance evaluation provides the coach with the necessary feedback about the effectiveness of his program as well. Continuous progress of most team members from test to test is an indication of a well-designed program and a highly motivated team. Additionally, the test scores provide a useful ranking of the athletes and can be used for selection of the team or starting players.

Setting team and individual goals   The establishment of goals and consequent training programs to achieve them is another strong form of motivation that leads to greater zest for training. There exist two types of goals: *individual goals* and *team goals*. Both are equally important. Initially, individual goals are more important since each individual really wants to see an improvement. He or she must see regular progress in order to want to continue; these goals, if well set, will allow progress to be seen.

To achieve team goals, a contribution is required from all team members. Just as with individual goals, there are team goals for each practice, each week, each month, each testing period, each tournament, and each season. They are usually discussed and determined at team meetings. Team discussion and team decisions increase both goal awareness and commitment. They produce a form of psychological contracting that binds the team to serious practice. Once set, team goals increase team unity and continuously exert strong social pressure upon all members to continue according to expectations since each member is an integral and necessary part of the whole.

Psychologists have suggested several guidelines that can be helpful in using goal-setting as a motivational tool.

(1) Goals should be *objective* and *specific* (attack efficiency should be 20%, improve speed-drill time by 8 seconds, improve the vertical jump by 2 centimetres, etc.) rather than general ("do your best," "try to improve by as much as you can," etc.);

(2) Goals should be *meaningful* (the player's vertical jump compares well – at the top – with the norms of his age group, etc.);

(3) Goals should be *obtainable* (realistic and yet demanding objectives – 50% chance of achievement – are the most effective goals for the player to strive for); and

MOTIVATION

(4) Goals should be *individualized* and should be based on past experience. The coach must know the athlete's abilities and limitations, as well as his aspiration levels. Only then can the coach formulate the athlete's realistic but challenging goals fairly accurately.

Final thought

It will be impossible for a coach to employ all of the motivational suggestions presented in this section. He may choose a few and build on them with ideas that may develop as he continues with his program. There are virtually no limits to the types of motivational ideas that can be developed and/or borrowed from other successful programs (not necessarily just from volleyball). However, every coach must also realize that no motivational procedure or strategy will have a lasting effect unless he knows how to teach correct volleyball skills and strategies, how to apply contemporary training methods, and how to work with athletes.

Inspirational slogans

To increase his motivational effectiveness the coach may use inspirational words and phrases that will get his team focused and motivated. Slogans for the day, week, or a specific game can be a useful tool. A small selection of inspiring slogans taken from *The Great Book of Inspiring Quotations*, a Sport Books Publisher publication, has been compiled in this section. The coach can select whichever quotations suit his or her team best.

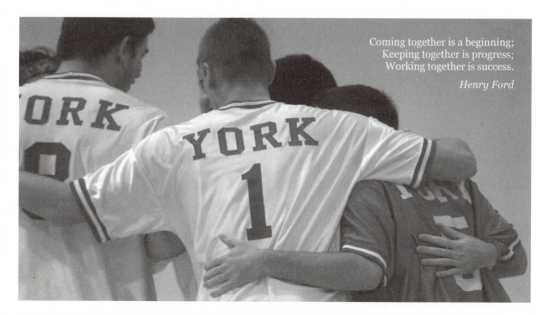

Coming together is a beginning;
Keeping together is progress;
Working together is success.

Henry Ford

LEAD-UP GAMES AND DRILLS

Ability

There is nothing more unequal than the equal treatment of unequals.
KEN BLANCHARD

Love means never having to say you're sorry ... and so does good execution.
ADAPTED FROM *LOVE STORY*

It's not how big you are, it's how big you play.
WALLY DYBA

Do the very best you can with what you have.
THEODORE ROOSEVELT

Don't measure what you should have accomplished with your ability.
JOHN WOODEN

There is hardly anybody good for everything, and there is scarcely anybody who is absolutely good for nothing.
LORD CHESTERFIELD

I am only one, but I am one. I cannot do everything, but I can do something. What I can do, I should do and, with the help of God, I will do!
EVERETT HALE

A ship in harbour is safe, but that is not what ships are built for.
ANONYMOUS

Perfection is the child of time.
JOSEPH HALL

A parrot talks much, but flies little.
ANONYMOUS

Everyone must row with the oars he has.
ENGLISH PROVERB

It is better to have little talent and much purpose than little purpose and much talent.
ANONYMOUS

Ability is nothing without opportunity.
NAPOLEON BONAPARTE

A diamond is a chunk of coal that made good under pressure.
ANONYMOUS

INSPIRATION

Attitude

Attitude is a little thing that makes a big difference.
ANONYMOUS

When you lose, say little. When you win, say less.
ANONYMOUS

Be a member of the DYBA family: **D**o **Y**our **B**est **A**lways.
WALLY DYBA

I could find the determination to keep on going. I learned that your mind can amaze your body, if you just keep telling yourself, I can do it, I can do it.
JON ERICKSON

Most of us are satisfied with so little in ourselves but demand so much from others.
ANONYMOUS

Good things happen to good people.
WALLY DYBA

Leadership is an attitude before it is an ability.
ANONYMOUS

Pride is a personal commitment. It is an attitude that separates excellence from mediocrity.
ANONYMOUS

Whether you think you can or think you can't – you are right.
HENRY FORD

It is more important than appearance, giftedness, or skill. It will make or break a company ... a home ... a team. The remarkable thing is we have a choice every day regarding the ATTITUDE we will embrace for that day. We cannot change our past, we cannot change the inevitable, but we can change our ATTITUDE.
ANONYMOUS

Life's battles don't always go to the stronger or faster man, but sooner or later the man who wins is the fellow who thinks he can.
ANONYMOUS

All things are possible to one who believes.
SAINT BERNARD OF CLAIRVAUX

LEAD-UP GAMES AND DRILLS

Character

Talent will get you to the top, but it takes character to keep you there.
JOHN WOODEN

No price is too high to pay for a good reputation.
ANONYMOUS

Sow an act, and you reap a habit. Sow a habit, and you reap a character. Sow a character, and you reap a destiny.
CHARLES READE

When we seek to discover the best in others, we somehow bring out the best in ourselves.
WILLIAM ARTHUR WARD

Following the path of least resistance is what makes rivers and men crooked.
ANONYMOUS

Nobody holds a good opinion of a man who has a low opinion of himself.
ANTHONY TROLLOPE

To get the true measure of a man, note how much more he does than is required of him.
ANONYMOUS

Those who are upset by criticism admit they deserve it.
CORNELIUS TACITUS

What lies behind us and what lies before us are tiny matters compared to what lies within us.
RALPH WALDO EMERSON

A man may make mistakes, but he isn't a failure until he starts blaming someone else.
JOHN WOODEN

The ultimate measure of a man is not where he stands in moments of comfort and convenience, but where he stands at times of challenge and controversy.
MARTIN LUTHER KING

The applause soon dies away, the prize is left behind, but the character you build up is yours forever.
ANONYMOUS

The best kind of pride is that which compels a man to do his very best work, even if no one is watching.
ANONYMOUS

INSPIRATION

Confidence

Experience tells you what to do; confidence allows you to do it.
STAN SMITH

He didn't know it couldn't be done ... so he did it.
ANONYMOUS

If you're prepared, then you're able to feel confident.
ROBERT J. RINGER

The only limit to our realization of tomorrow will be our doubts of today.
FRANKLIN D. ROOSEVELT

Fear is your best friend or your worst enemy. It's like fire. If you can control it, it can cook for you; it can heat your house. If you can't control it, it will burn you every time.
CUS D'AMATO

Do not attempt to do a thing unless you are sure of yourself; but do not relinquish it simply because someone else is not sure of you.
STEWART E. WHITE

In order to succeed, we must first believe we can.
MICHAEL KORDA

Courage

None but a coward dares to boast that he has never known fear.
FERDINAND FOCH

We should never let our fears hold us back from pursuing our hopes.
JOHN F. KENNEDY

If a man never fails, it may be because he never tries.
ANONYMOUS

Life only demands from you the strength you possess. Only one feat is possible – not to have run away.
DAG HAMMARSKJOLD

Fortune sides with him who dares.
VIRGIL

Courage is very important. Like a muscle, it is strengthened by use.
RUTH GORDON

Everyone has talent. What is rare is the courage to follow the talent to the dark place where it leads.
ERICA JONG

LEAD-UP GAMES AND DRILLS

Effort

Always begin somewhere. You cannot build a reputation on what you intend to do.
ANONYMOUS

The best angle from which to approach any problem is the *try*-angle.
ANONYMOUS

To try to be better is to be better.
CHARLOTTE CUSHMAN

Your rewards in life are always in direct proportion to your contribution.
ANONYMOUS

Never discourage anyone who makes progress, no matter how slow.
PLATO

If one has not given everything, one has given nothing.
GEORGES GUYNEMER

It doesn't take any ability to hustle.
BILLY MARTIN

Leadership

Learn to obey before you command.
SOLON

Great leaders were first great followers.
ANONYMOUS

He that would govern others, first should be the master of himself.
PHILIP MASSINGER

Leadership is action, not position.
DONALD H. MCGANNON

A good leader takes a little more than his share of blame; a little less than his share of credit.
ARNOLD H. GLASGOW

Nothing is more difficult, and therefore more precious, than to be able to decide.
NAPOLEON BONAPARTE

Anyone can hold the helm when the sea is calm.
PUBLILIUS SYRUS

INSPIRATION

Persistence

Defeat doesn't finish a man – quit does. A man is not finished when he's defeated. He's finished when he quits.
RICHARD NIXON

Top cats often begin as underdogs.
BERNARD MELTZER

The drop of rain maketh a hole in the stone, not by violence, but by oft falling.
BISHOP HUGH LATIMER

A man of destiny knows that beyond this hill lies another and another. The journey is never complete.
F. W. DE KLERK

Man is not made for defeat. A man can be destroyed but not defeated.
ERNEST HEMINGWAY

No man is defeated without until he has first been defeated within.
ELEANOR ROOSEVELT

Failure is the line of least persistence.
ANONYMOUS

Practice

It takes twenty years to become an overnight success.
EDDIE CANTOR

Practice makes perfect, so be careful what you practice.
ANONYMOUS

A gem cannot be polished without friction, nor man perfected without trials.
ANONYMOUS

Failure to prepare certainly means preparing to fail.
JOHN WOODEN

Remember the five P's: proper preparation prevents poor performance.
ANONYMOUS

I will get ready, and then perhaps my chance will come.
ABRAHAM LINCOLN

Everyone has the will to win, but few have the will to prepare to win.
BOBBY KNIGHT

LEAD-UP GAMES AND DRILLS

Success

Success ... simple things done well, consistently.
WALLY DYBA

Success is not so much achievement as achieving. Refuse to join the cautious crowd that plays not to lose – play to win.
DAVID J. MAHONEY

He who does not hope to win has already lost.
JOSÉ JOAQUÍN OLMEDO

Success is to be measured not so much by the position that one has reached as by the obstacles that one has overcome while trying to succeed.
MARK TWAIN

A winner respects those who are superior to him and tries to learn something from them; a loser resents those who are superior to him and tries to find chinks in their armour.
ANONYMOUS

A winner feels responsible for more than his job; a loser says, "I only work here."
ANONYMOUS

A minute's success pays the failure of years.
ROBERT BROWNING

A winner works harder than a loser and has more time; a loser is always too busy to do what is necessary.
ANONYMOUS

Over the years, I have become convinced that every detail is important and that success usually accompanies attention to little details. It is this, in my judgment, that makes for the difference between champion and near champion.
JOHN WOODEN

Only a mediocre person is always at his best.
SOMERSET MAUGHAM

Give the world the best you have and the best will come back to you.
ANONYMOUS

Fame is what others give you. Success is what you give yourself.
ANONYMOUS

INSPIRATION

Teamwork

Coming together is a beginning; keeping together is progress; working together is success.
HENRY FORD

Nothing is impossible for the man who does not have to do it himself.
EARL WILSON

Teamwork is the fuel that allows common people to attain uncommon results.
ANONYMOUS

Teamwork divides the tasks and doubles the successes.
ANONYMOUS

It's amazing what a team can accomplish when no one cares who gets the credit.
JOHN WOODEN

Together
Everyone
Achieves
More
ANONYMOUS

Alone we can do so little; together we can do so much.
HELEN KELLER

Wisdom

The only real mistake is the one from which we learn nothing.
JOHN POWELL

Whenever you fall, pick up something.
OSWALD THEODORE AVERY

Experience is not what happens to a man. It is what a man does with what happens to him.
ALDOUS HUXLEY

Learn from the mistakes of others – you can never live long enough to make them all yourself.
ANONYMOUS

Some folks are wise, and some are otherwise.
TOBIAS SMOLLETT

A man should never be ashamed to own he has been in the wrong, which is but saying, in other words, that he is wiser today than he was yesterday.
ALEXANDER POPE

When all is said and done, as a rule, more is said than done.
LOU HOLTZ

PART III

OBJECTIVES OF THE GAME OF VOLLEYBALL *35*

VOLLEYBALL RULE CHANGES AND ADDITIONS *36*

BASIC VOLLEYBALL CONCEPTS *38*

THE BASIC VOLLEYBALL PLAY (BVP) *40*

DEVELOPING AN UNDERSTANDING OF THE BASIC VOLLEYBALL CONCEPTS *42*
- The one-on-one situation *43*
- The two-on-two situation *46*
- The four-on-four situation *48*
- The five-on-five situation *54*
- The six-on-six situation *58*
- Service reception formations *60*
- Team play worksheet *73*

HOW TO PLAY THE GAME

The game of volleyball can trace its origins back to 1895 in the United States, but the sport is only now beginning to attain the same type of popularity in North America it has enjoyed worldwide for decades. Today, more than 24 million Americans and over 800 million players worldwide play volleyball at least once a week, ranking it second behind only soccer in participation rates among all sports.

Over the last decade, volleyball has witnessed unprecedented growth to become one of the big five international sports. The International Volleyball Federation (FIVB), with its 218 affiliated national federations, is now the largest international sporting federation in the world.

Objectives of the game of volleyball

Volleyball is a sport played by two teams on a playing court divided by a net. The objectives of the game for each team are to send the ball over the net in an attempt to ground it on the opponent's court, and to prevent the ball from being grounded on its own court. Every action in the sport should relate to these objectives. Each team is allowed three contacts to return the ball over the net (in addition to the ball being contacted on the block).

The ball is put into play by the right backcourt player, who serves the ball over the net into the opponent's court. A player is not allowed to contact the ball twice consecutively, except when attempting a block. The rally continues until the ball touches the floor, goes out of bounds, or is not successfully returned into the opponent's court.

A team wins a set by scoring 25 points with a minimum 2-point advantage, and wins a match by winning a best of three or best of five sets. A deciding set is played to 15 points with a 2-point advantage. There is no point cap.

Basic objectives of the game
1. Ground the ball on your opponent's court.
2. Prevent the ball from being grounded on your own court.

HOW TO PLAY THE GAME

Volleyball rule changes and additions

Although the basic rules of the game are outlined in the FIVB rulebook, many of the rules have been modified, depending on the age of participants, the jurisdiction of the competition, or even the country of play. Coaches and athletes should be aware of the differences between the rules that govern their particular competitions and those of the FIVB. It should also be noted that many of the FIVB rules have changed significantly in the past decade. Some of the most significant changes are outlined here.

Let serve (2000)   If a served ball touches the net and then crosses the net to the opponent's court within the crossing space, there is a continuation of play.

This rule change was intended to speed up play and increase spectator excitement.

The libero player (1999)   The libero is a backcourt specialist whose primary functions are to play backcourt defence and/or pass the serve. The libero is restricted to performing as a backcourt player and has no right to serve, block, attempt to block, complete an attack, or hand set a ball on or in front of the attack line to a teammate. In addition, the libero must wear a different coloured shirt than the other members of the team.

Substitutions involving a libero are unlimited in number and are not counted as regular substitutions. A libero can only be replaced by the player she substituted for. Before the libero can reenter for a different player, one rally has to be completed. Libero substitutions can only occur while the ball is out of play and before the whistle for service. A libero cannot take part in normal substitutions.

The libero player rule was introduced in an effort to increase rally length through increased defensive digging. It is also believed that the libero rule will allow shorter players an opportunity to play the game at the highest levels.

Side-out scoring to rally-point scoring (1999)   In *side-out scoring*, a point is awarded only to the serving team when it wins the rally. When the receiving team wins the rally, no point is scored; the receiving team gains the right to serve, and its players rotate one position clockwise. Rotation ensures that players play both at the net and in the back zone of the court (except the libero player).

In *rally-point scoring*, a point is awarded to the team that wins the rally, regardless of which team served the ball. When the receiving team wins the rally, in addition to scoring a point, it gains the right to serve. Its players then rotate one position clockwise.

The change from side-out scoring to rally-point scoring was made to more effectively define the time parameters of a set. In side-out scoring, set length could range from 10 minutes to well over an hour. This made live television coverage of volleyball matches difficult to schedule.

Coloured ball (1999)   A new coloured ball (blue, yellow, and white panels) became

RULE CHANGES

the exclusive game ball for all official FIVB competitions in 1999. The unique design and colour combination are registered trademarks of the FIVB. For National Collegiate Athletic Association (NCAA) competitions, the ball panels are red, white, and blue, while in Canadian Interuniversity Sport (CIS) competitions, they are red, white, and black.

The coloured ball was introduced to enhance spectator appeal in addition to allowing the athletes to track the ball more effectively in matches.

The service zone (1995)   The service zone consists of a 9-metre-wide area beyond the end line of the court (the end line excluded). The lateral boundaries of this zone are marked by two 15-centimetre-long lines, drawn 20 centimetres behind the end line as an extension of the sidelines. Both lines are included in the width of the zone (see Figure 3.1).

The serving player is exempt from the positional order rule. The server may be at the left of the players in positions 5 or 6. All other players on the court must remain in correct order.

The ball may touch any part of the body (1995)   In the past, players were not allowed to contact the ball below the knee. Now, players may contact the ball with any part of the body, including the feet, except for the serve. The serve must still be carried out with one hand or any part of the arm.

Liberalization of ball contact judgements (1995)   The liberalization of ball contact judgements has minimized the impact of referees during competitive matches. This rule has allowed the athletes to play and decide the outcome of rallies without the referee making a subjective judgement on the quality of the contact.

Ball contacts previously judged as "held balls" are still considered a fault, with the exception of balls played in defensive actions. Similarly a "double contact" is still a fault, except in cases where the player makes a spectacular effort. On the first ball contact by a player of one team, the ball may touch different parts of the body consecutively, provided it occurs during the same action.

Referees must now judge ball contacts in a more liberalized manner.

Summary of recent rule changes

- Let serve
- The libero player
- Rally-point scoring
- Coloured ball
- Widening of the service zone
- Ball contact with any part of the body
- Liberalization of ball contacts

HOW TO PLAY THE GAME

Basic volleyball concepts

Five basic concepts are fundamental to understanding the game of volleyball: offence, defence, service, service reception, and transition.

Offence   Offence in volleyball is related to the first outlined objective: an attempt by one team to ground the ball on the opponent's court.

A team is generally thought to be on offence when the ball is on its side of the net. Offence usually begins with the first ball contact and ends with an attack. However, if the first ball contact is not controlled, every effort is made to (1) keep the ball off the floor and (2) try to set up an attack. Thus, **a team is on offence when it has control of the ball**.

Defence   Defence in volleyball is related to the second outlined objective: an attempt to prevent the ball from being grounded on its own court.

A team is generally thought to be on defence when the ball is in the opponent's court. However, if the ball is not controlled on its own side, a team initially puts its efforts into preventing the ball from hitting the floor, then controlling it or sending it over to the opponent's side. Thus, **a team is on defence when it does not have control of the ball**.

Service   The serve can be viewed as the act of putting the ball in play. Indeed many coaches at the younger levels stress to their athletes to "just get the ball over the net." However, putting the ball in play is not one of the prime objectives of the game. The serve is the first opportunity at scoring a point, and a well-placed serve can minimize the effectiveness of an opponent's attack. It should also be noted that at service, the ball is totally under the control of the server. Therefore, **service is an integral part of the offence**.

Service reception   Service reception is widely considered the most important aspect of the game of volleyball. It is the act of receiving the serve and initiating the offence. Initially, service reception can be viewed as a defensive alignment against the offence of the serve. If the ball is not controlled, the team makes every attempt to keep the ball off the floor and put it over the net within three contacts. If the ball is controlled, the team then initiates an offence, culminating in an attack. Thus, **service reception is the act of receiving the serve, and if the ball is controlled, initiating the offence**.

Transition   Transition can be described as the movement from one phase of the game to another, that is, from offence to defence and vice versa. This is clearly illustrated within the concept of service reception.

Initially, service reception is a defensive manoeuvre or phase, as a team must defend

BASIC VOLLEYBALL CONCEPTS

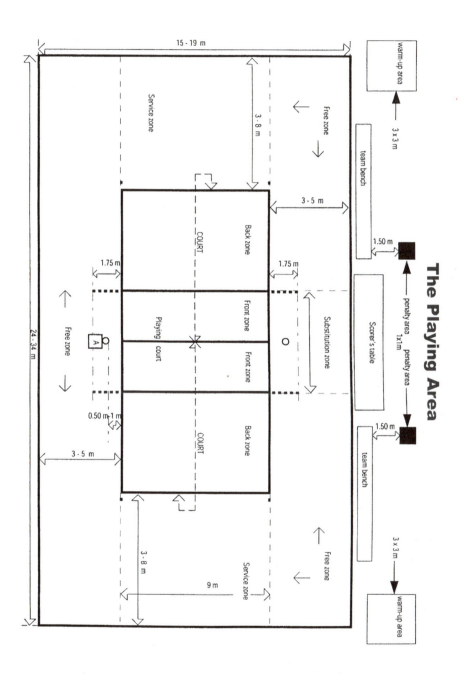

Figure 3.1 The volleyball court and playing area layout and dimensions.

HOW TO PLAY THE GAME

against an offensive action, the serve. If the ball is controlled after service, then the team now is involved in running the offence. Once the offence has been completed and thus control of the ball relinquished, the team is once again in a defensive phase. These team play phases or transitions are considered the ***basic cycle of actions*** (see Figure 3.2).

Summary of basic volleyball concepts

1. **Offence:** a team is on offence when it has control of the ball.

2. **Defence:** a team is on defence when it does not have control of the ball.

3. **Service:** act of putting the ball in play. The first chance at offence.

4. **Service reception:** act of receiving the serve. If the ball is controlled, the offence is initiated.

5. **Transition:** changes from one phase of the game to another.
   - service to defence
   - service reception to offence
   - defence to offence
   - offence to defence

The basic volleyball play (BVP)

In accordance with the objectives of the game, "getting the ball over the net" is not a prime objective. Many a time, this is the end result when a team cannot control the ball to mount an effective attack. Thus "getting the ball over the net" should be used as a last resort.

Many novice volleyball players utilize this tactic – whoever touches the ball immediately sends it over the net. Unfortunately, this tactic has proven to be somewhat successful, as novice athletes generally do not have the skill set to control the ball and mount a successful attack. It is imperative that novice volleyball players be ingrained in the notion that volleyball is a unique net sport where three contacts in a basic volleyball play is the expectation.

It is important to have an exact understanding of the elements in the basic volleyball play. Many believe that the basic volleyball play is "bump, set, spike," and in general terms, this is correct. However, given the more liberal passing rules and given what a team is actually attempting to accomplish, a three-contact view of the basic volleyball play should be adopted: (1) on first contact the ball should be passed **to the net**; (2) on

BASIC VOLLEYBALL CONCEPTS

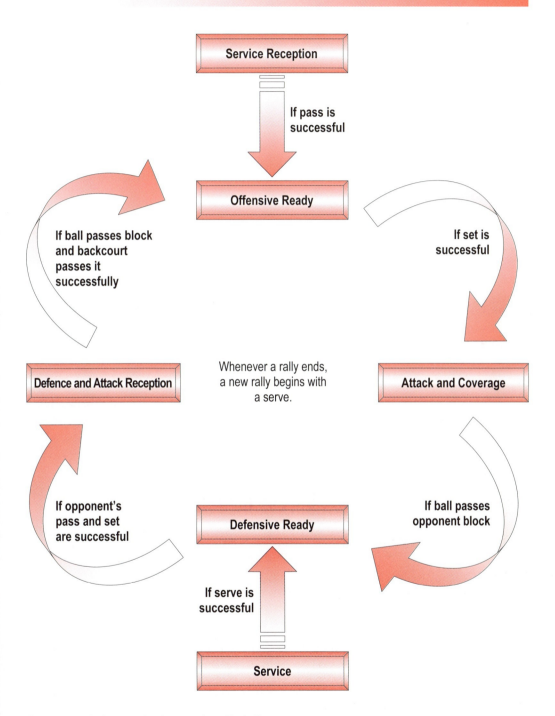

Figure 3.2 The basic cycle of actions for volleyball.

HOW TO PLAY THE GAME

second contact the ball should be passed **at the net**; (3) on third contact the ball should be directed **over the net**.

On first contact, the ball that is passed to the net should be directed with a reasonably high arc to the middle front.

On second contact, the ball should be directed at the net with a reasonably high arc to the outside corner of the net – either to the left front or to the right front. The second contact is usually called a *set*. In a situation where the first ball is not successfully directed to the middle front of the net, the second ball should still be directed (set) to either outside corner of the net. The second ball contact is very important in the basic volleyball play, especially if the first pass is errant. All athletes must be able to pass (set) the ball with a reasonably high arc to the outside corner of the net.

The third contact involves directing the ball over the net.

The basic volleyball play

To the net, at the net (outside), over the net.

1. On first contact, the ball should be passed **to the net**.
2. On second contact, the ball should be passed (set) **at the net**, to the **outside corner**.
3. On third contact, the ball should be directed **over the net**.

Developing an understanding of the basic volleyball concepts

The simplest way to develop an understanding of the basic volleyball concepts is to explore them in an artificial one-on-one situation. Since some individuals may not be proficient at all of the individual volleyball skills, a toss-catch adaptation of the passing skills should be used.

For the *forearm pass*, the ball should be caught below the waistline with two hands, arms fully extended. The toss should be executed in a similar fashion. Holding the ball with both hands, arms fully extended, the shoulders rotate upward and forward so that the ball is released in the direction of the target. This toss-catch action closely mimics the actual action of the forearm pass.

BASIC VOLLEYBALL CONCEPTS

For the *volley pass*, the hands should be held in a similar shape as for the actual volley pass. The hands should be slightly above the head, the thumbs and index fingers of both hands (while barely touching) forming a triangle, with the rest of the fingers spread to make a bowl shape. The ball can be caught or allowed to rest in the bowl. The toss is made by extending the elbows and directing the ball upward and toward the intended target. Again, this toss-catch action closely mimics the actual action of the volley pass.

At no time should an athlete be allowed to catch a ball utilizing the forearm pass adaptation and then toss it utilizing the volley pass adaptation or vice versa.

Toss-catch adaptations of passing skills

Forearm pass: arms fully extended, waist level, palms facing each other, thumbs up
- Ball is caught at waist height, with arms fully extended.
- Ball is tossed by a rotation of the shoulders.

Volley pass: hands slightly above the forehead, bowl shaped, thumbs down
- Ball is caught above the forehead with elbows bent.
- Ball is tossed by extension of the elbows.

The one-on-one situation

Two athletes begin by standing on either side of the net. The court dimensions should be reduced in size to no more than 2 metres wide and 6 metres deep on either side of the net.

Cooperative play

Initial play is cooperative, and emphasis is placed on using three contacts on a side, employing the forearm pass and volley pass toss-catch adaptations only. The basic volleyball play of "to the net, at the net, and over the net" and associated movements should also be stressed.

To initiate play, one individual (A), standing behind the attack line, tosses the ball up in the air and executes a forearm pass toss-catch adaptation to direct the ball **to the net** (Diagram 1A).

HOW TO PLAY THE GAME

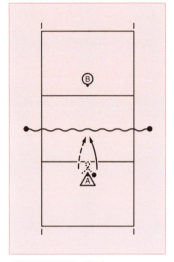
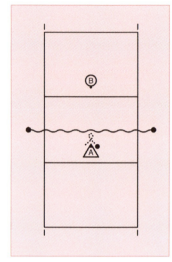
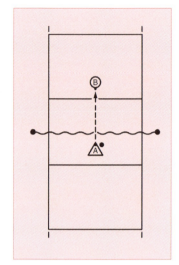

Diagram 1A To the net.   *Diagram 1B* At the net.   *Diagram 1C* Over the net.

At the net, he executes either the forearm or volley pass toss-catch adaptation and directs the ball so that he can play it himself (Diagram 1B).

Utilizing the volley pass adaptation, he then directs the ball **over the net** to his partner (B), who is standing behind the attack line on the other side of the net (Diagram 1C).

Player A then runs backward to his initial position behind the attack line, while player B utilizes the appropriate three contacts of the basic volleyball play (**to the net**, **at the net**, and **over the net**).

This series of actions is repeated. Ideally the first pass should be a forearm pass adaptation and the last pass a volley pass adaptation. The second pass can be either pass adaptation.

This one-on-one cooperative play continues until both player A and player B are relatively adept at utilizing the forearm and volley pass toss-catch adaptations, moving to and from the net and employing the basic volleyball play, consisting of "**to the net**, **at the net**, and **over the net**." At this point a "hot potato" element should be added to the toss-catch adaptations, which involves catching the ball and then immediately releasing it. This "hot potato" element further shapes the speed of the toss-catch pass adaptations to more closely approximate the actual speed of the forearm and volley passes. With very little specific instruction given for the actual forearm and volley passes, athletes can liberally use these skills in this cooperative play.

In this cooperative situation, with guidance from the coach or instructor, the athletes can also develop a better understanding of the basic volleyball concepts.

BASIC VOLLEYBALL CONCEPTS

Competitive play

Competitive one-on-one play is similar to the cooperative play, except that each athlete actually tries to ground the ball on the opponent's court (win the rally). The court dimensions are expanded to approximately 3 metres wide and 9 metres deep on each side of the net. In this competitive scenario, a ball landing inside the attack line (from the centre line to the 3-metre line) is considered out of bounds.

Play is initiated with a self-toss, and three contacts are required per side during each rally. The "hot potato" toss-catch adaptations, the actual volley and forearm pass skills, or any combination of these can be used in the rally, but the ball must be contacted with two hands or two arms. Failure to do so is considered a ball-handling fault, and the rally is terminated. Play continues to a predetermined score or until the coach or instructor stops play.

Knowledge check

Once players have had an opportunity to play competitively for a while, they should be able to answer the following questions.

Q: What ability do individuals who win during competitive play possess above all?

A: Control

Q: What elementary offensive tactics can be employed to make it more difficult for the opponent to control the ball?

A:
- Ball placement
- Ball speed
- Ball trajectory

Q: What elements make playing defence more successful?

A:
- Court positioning
- Movement ability
- "Reading" the opposition

HOW TO PLAY THE GAME

The two-on-two situation

The two-on-two situation more closely resembles the game of volleyball, as the ball is passed to and received from another individual. Actually, the ball is passed to a target area rather than to a player per se. The nonpasser must move to this target (or where the ball is passed to) in order to make the next play.

The court dimensions for two-on-two play should be approximately 4.5 metres wide and 9 metres deep on each side of the net. Again, a ball landing inside the attack line (from the centre line to the 3-metre line) is considered out of bounds. On each side of the court, two players start side by side (parallel to the net), approximately 6 metres away from the net. Initially, the toss-catch variations for the forearm pass and volley pass should be used.

Cooperative play

Players on each team stand parallel to the net, approximately 6 metres away from the net (Diagram 2A). To initiate play, one player (A) tosses the ball up in the air and then executes a forearm pass toss-catch adaptation, directing the ball **to the net**. The ball should be passed with a reasonably high arc to the net, approximately at the midpoint between the two sidelines. When player A tosses the ball up, player B should begin moving into position at the net for the next play (Diagram 2B). Although a perfect pass should go to the middle front position on the court, player B must be prepared to track the ball wherever it goes and beat it to the spot.

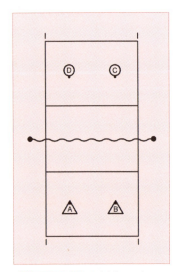

Diagram 2A Initial starting positions.

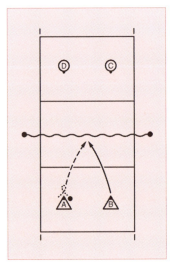

Diagram 2B Passing the ball to the net.

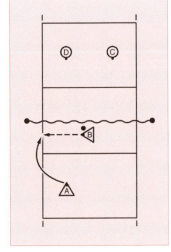

Diagram 2C Passing the ball at the net to the corner.

BASIC VOLLEYBALL CONCEPTS

For the second pass, player B should stand with shoulders perpendicular to the net. She should preferably use the volley pass toss-catch adaptation to direct the ball **at the net, to the corner** with a reasonable arc to the sideline closest to player A, approximately half a metre away from the net. After playing the ball to the net for player B, player A should begin moving toward the sideline at the net in preparation to meet the ball passed by player B (Diagram 2C). The final play on the ball is made by player A, who directs the ball **over the net** to the opposing team.

Once the ball has been directed over the net, player A and player B runs backward to their starting positions, watching the play develop on the other side of the net.

When the ball is played over the net, player C and player D must react from their defensive positions (side by side, parallel to the net, approximately 6 metres away from the net), quickly deciding who will make the first contact. Once one player has committed to making the first contact, the other player must begin moving toward the net and the middle front target area.

The player (C or D) making the first contact executes a forearm pass toss-catch adaptation (preferred) or volley pass toss-catch adaptation and directs the ball **to the net** toward the target area. The same sequence of actions described previously for players A and B occurs between players C and D, with the player making the first contact also making the third and final contact to direct the ball over the net. This sequence of actions continues until the ball is grounded or one team is unable to return the ball over the net within three contacts. The team winning the rally reinitiates play.

Aspects of the game that are stressed during two-on-two cooperative play

Decision making

- who will play the ball on the first contact
- who will move to the net for the second contact

Movement patterns

- movement to the net and away from the net
- beating the ball to the spot to pass it to the outside corner
- meeting the ball to direct it over the net

Identifying appropriate targets

- targets are designated areas on the court, not where individual players are standing

HOW TO PLAY THE GAME

The four-on-four situation

Once the athletes are familiar with the decision-making and movement requirements of the two-on-two situation, they advance to the four-on-four situation, which serves as an effective springboard to full six-on-six team play. Unlike the two-on-two situation, four-on-four games can be played on a full volleyball court. Balls landing inside the attack line are no longer considered out of bounds.

Starting positions for four-on-four are roughly the four corners of the court (Diagram 3A). The frontcourt players begin at the net approximately 1 metre in from each sideline. The two backcourt players begin approximately 2 metres in from the end line and 1 metre in from each sideline. The player beginning in the right back position is designated as player 1, the right front position as player 2, the left front position as player 4, and the left back position as player 5. These numbers correspond to player positions when playing six-on-six (Diagram 3B). The middle front (player 3) and the middle back (player 6) positions are omitted.

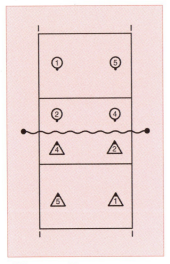

Diagram 3A Starting positions for four-on-four.

Positions on a Volleyball Court

1. Right back
2. Right front
3. Middle front
4. Left front
5. Left back
6. Middle back

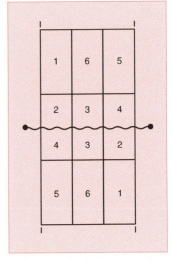

Diagram 3B Zones on a volleyball court.

Four-on-four play allows players to gain knowledge of and practice the five basic volleyball concepts (see page 38) in a simplified environment. Players really have only two choices to make. Players in the frontcourt, depending on which side of the court the ball is sent over the net, either stay in their relative starting positions or back away from the net to the attack line. Players in the backcourt either stay in their relative starting positions or move sideways 1 to 2 metres into the court parallel to the end line. Players must make these positional adjustments to maximize their court coverage and prevent the ball from being grounded on their own court.

BASIC VOLLEYBALL CONCEPTS

Movement choices, frontcourt

1. Stay to defend at the net.
2. Move back to the attack line in better position to prevent the ball from being grounded.

Movement choices, backcourt

1. Stay to defend the line attack.
2. Move into the court to defend the cross-court attack.

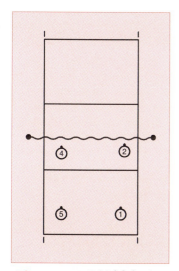

Diagram 4A Initial defensive positions.

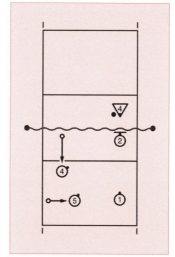

Diagram 4B Defensive movements with ball sent over net from position 4 (left side of court).

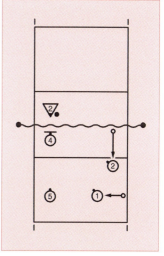

Diagram 4C Defensive movements with ball sent over net from position 2 (right side of court).

Once the appropriate defensive movements have been made and the ball is sent over, the players must quickly decide who is the primary digger and who are the support diggers.

The *primary digger* is the player in the best position to prevent the ball from being grounded. This player makes the first contact in attempting to control the ball and initiate

HOW TO PLAY THE GAME

the offence. The remaining players on the team are **support diggers** who attempt to play and control the ball on the second contact if the primary digger is unable to effectively control the ball.

Primary digger controls the ball

If the primary digger is able to control the ball, the basic volleyball play is initiated. On first contact by the primary digger, the ball is directed to the net with a high arc to the middle frontcourt position. Unless he is the primary digger, the player in position 1 must beat the ball to this target for the second play on the ball. This player then sets the ball outside to either sideline. Ideally, this set should be high and travel out to the sideline, about 1 metre away from the net.

The player in position 1 is the designated setter in this situation. When a player moves from the backcourt to the frontcourt to set the ball, there is a backcourt setter. This is a **penetrating setter** system.

> **Penetrating setter:** A player moving from the backcourt to the frontcourt to set the ball.

Once the primary digger has made the first contact, frontcourt players in positions 2 and 4 should immediately move to their initial attack positions (the sidelines at the attack line) and prepare to attack the ball on the third contact. When the ball is set to a frontcourt player, the remaining players surround the attacker defensively in case the ball is blocked.

Once the ball has been sent over the net, players return to their initial defensive positions as the other team attempts to execute its own basic volleyball play.

Both primary and secondary diggers must maintain focus in order to successfully control the ball.

BASIC VOLLEYBALL CONCEPTS

Ball attacked from position 4

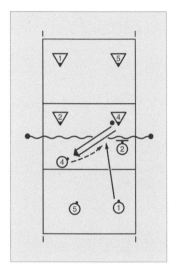
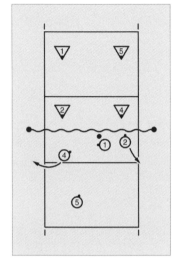
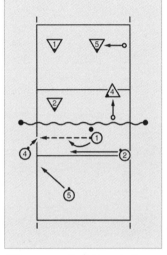

Diagram 5A Primary digger passes ball to net, high middle. Setter moves to beat the ball.

Diagram 5B Frontcourt players move to their initial attack positions.

Diagram 5C Setter sets the ball high outside. Others surround the attacker. Defenders make appropriate defensive movements.

Primary digger in position 5 and attacker in position 2 is set

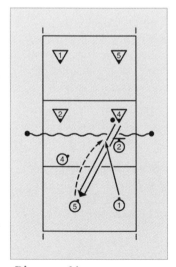
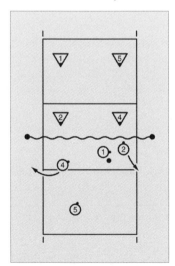
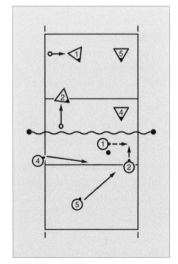

Diagram 6A

Diagram 6B

Diagram 6C

51

HOW TO PLAY THE GAME

Primary digger in position 2 and attacker in position 4 is set

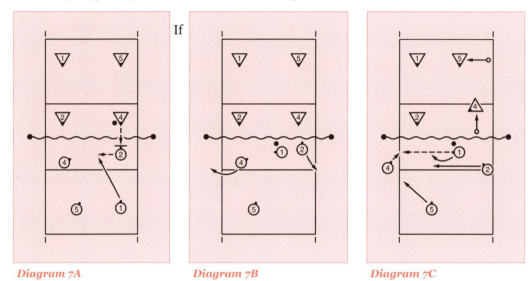

Diagram 7A   Diagram 7B   Diagram 7C

Primary digger in position 1

The player in position 1 is the primary digger and the ball is controlled, the basic volleyball play is initiated. However, in this case, the player in position 1 calls out "Help" to alert the secondary setter, the player in position 2, that she must set the ball on the second contact (Diagram 8A–C).

On the first contact, the ball is directed to the net, with a high arc to the middle frontcourt position. The player in position 2 must beat the ball to this target and set the ball outside to the left sideline. Again, the set should be high and travel out to the left sideline, about 1 metre away from the net.

The remainder of the basic volleyball play is executed, and once the ball has been sent over the net, players return to their initial defensive positions and prepare to defend the opponent's attack.

In the situation where the player in position 1 digs the ball, the player in position 2 becomes the designated setter. This player is a *nonpenetrating setter*. If the player in position 2 was assigned the responsibilities of the designated setter regardless of who the primary digger was, the system of play would be called a nonpenetrating system.

Nonpenetrating setter: A player from the frontcourt who sets the ball.

BASIC VOLLEYBALL CONCEPTS

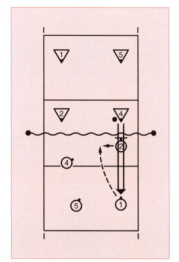
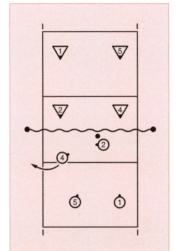
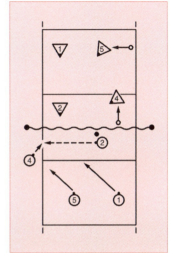

Diagram 8A Primary digger is the setter in position 1 and passes the ball to the net, high middle. The secondary setter in position 2 moves to beat the ball.

Diagram 8B Frontcourt players move to their initial attack positions.

Diagram 8C Secondary setter sets the ball high outside. Others surround the attacker. Defenders make appropriate defensive movements.

Primary digger does not control the ball

If the primary digger is unable to control the ball, the remaining players on the court must quickly decide who is in the best position to control the ball on the second contact. This player must get into position to set the ball high and outside to either sideline, rather than to the middle of the court. The sideline chosen for the set depends on the best angle for the outside player to attack the ball on the third contact. If possible, the frontcourt players should begin moving to their initial attack positions off the net before the set is made. Again, players should surround the attacker defensively in case the ball is blocked.

Once the ball has been sent over the net, players return to their initial defensive positions as the other team attempts to execute its own basic volleyball play.

HOW TO PLAY THE GAME

The five-on-five situation

The foundation for team play has been established with the four-on-four situation. By adding a fifth player on a side, shaping of full team play can continue. The fifth player can be placed as the backcourt player in position 6 or the frontcourt player in position 3. Regardless of the system of play, basic defensive movement patterns remain the same; however, responsibilities may differ. The basic movement pattern of players in position 3 or position 6 from their initial defensive positions is to "follow the ball," moving parallel to the net.

The basic movement pattern of players in either position 3 or position 6 is to follow the ball, with movement parallel to the net.

Basic defensive systems of play

1. **6-up defence** – nonpenetrating setter in position 2
2. **6-back defence** – nonpenetrating setter in position 2
3. **6-up defence** – nonpenetrating setter in position 3
4. **6-back defence** – nonpenetrating setter in position 3
5. **6-up defence** – penetrating setter in position 6
6. **6-back defence** – penetrating setter in position 1

BASIC VOLLEYBALL CONCEPTS

Adding fifth player in backcourt (position 6) or frontcourt (position 3)

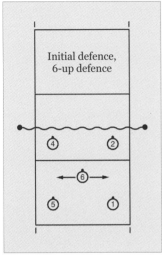
Diagram 9A

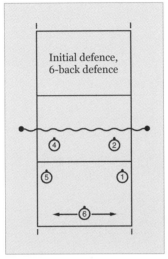
Diagram 9B

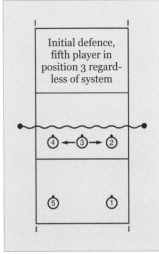
Diagram 9C

Example 1 Defensive movements with attack from opponent's position 4 (left front), followed by transition movements to attack. Utilizing 6-up defence with setter in position 6.

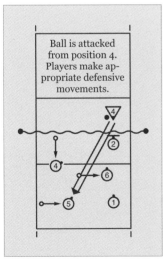
Diagram 10A

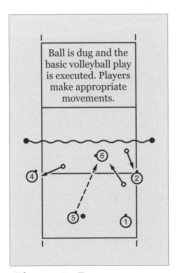
Diagram 10B

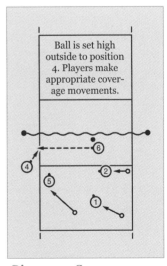
Diagram 10C

HOW TO PLAY THE GAME

Example 2 Defensive movements with attack from opponent's position 2 (right front), followed by transition movements to attack. Utilizing 6-back defence with setter in position 1.

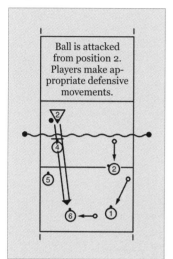

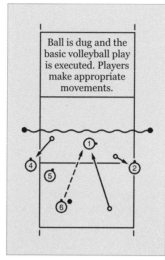

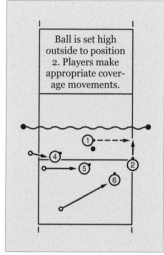

Diagram 11A   *Diagram 11B*   *Diagram 11C*

Example 3 Defensive movements with attack from opponent's position 4 (left front), followed by transition movements to attack. Utilizing player in position 3 as a middle blocker and setter.

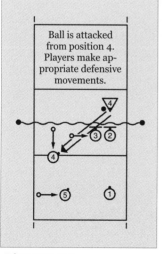

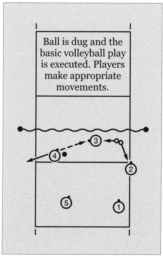

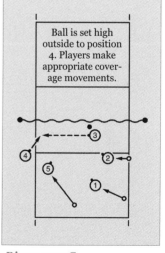

Diagram 12A   *Diagram 12B*   *Diagram 12C*

BASIC VOLLEYBALL CONCEPTS

Player in position 3 as a middle blocker and attacker

When the player in position 3 is to be used as a middle blocker and middle attacker, the transition movement after the attacked ball goes past him is very specific. The middle blocker/attacker must clear out of the middle front position at the net and go to the *middle blocker attack ready position*. This position is located at the attack line, about 1.5 metres in from the left sideline.

This movement clears the area in the middle front position for the designated setter to get the first pass that goes to the net. It also is the movement that prepares the middle blocker to approach for a middle attack.

There must also be a slight adjustment to the first pass. The first pass still goes to the net but must be more controlled in order to go between the middle front and right front positions.

When the setter comes from position 2, the set (or second pass) can go high outside to the sideline in position 4 or high in the middle (position 3). When the setter comes from position 1, the set can go high to either sideline (position 2 or position 4) or high in the middle (position 3). The latter situation incorporates a three-attacker system.

Middle blocker/attacker systems

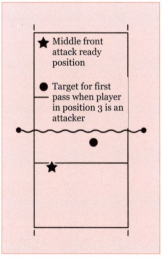

Diagram 13A

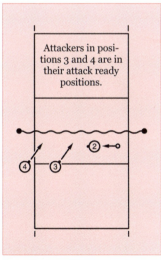

Diagram 13B

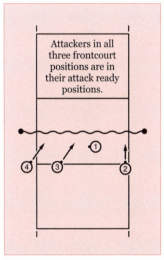

Diagram 13C

HOW TO PLAY THE GAME

The six-on-six situation

Combining the five-on-five situations where the fifth player is frontcourt or backcourt leads to the six-on-six situation. No new movements or responsibilities are incorporated.

Example 1   6-up defence – nonpenetrating setter in position 2

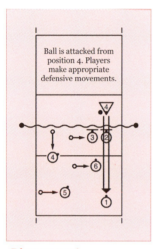

Diagram 14A

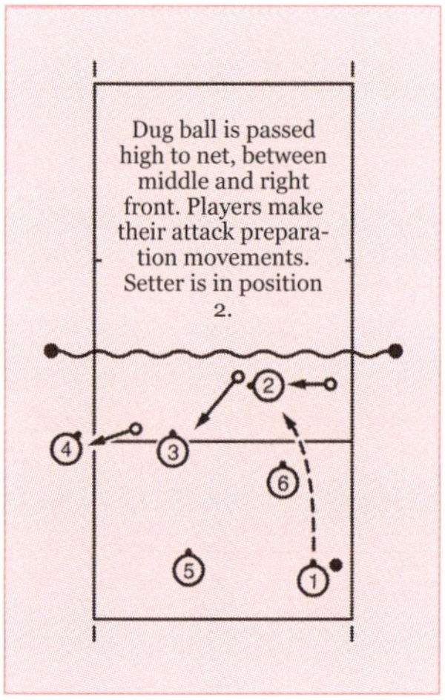

Diagram 14B

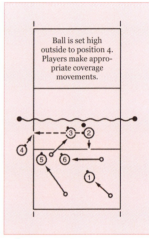

Diagram 14C

Example 2   6-back defence – nonpenetrating setter in position 3

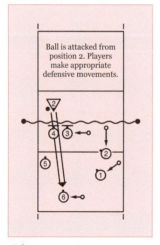

Diagram 15A

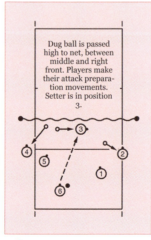

Diagram 15B

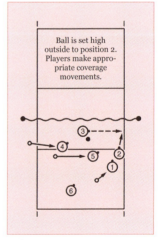

Diagram 15C

BASIC VOLLEYBALL CONCEPTS

Example 3 6-up defence – penetrating setter in position 6

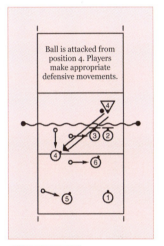
Diagram 16A

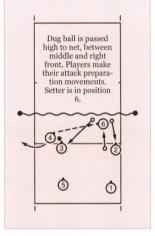
Diagram 16B

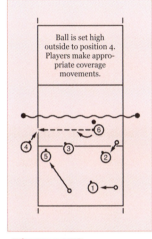
Diagram 16C

Example 4 6-back defence – penetrating setter in position 1

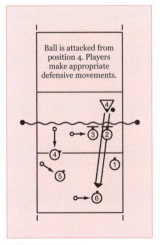
Diagram 17A

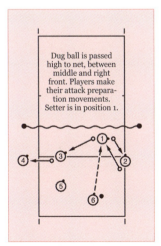
Diagram 17B

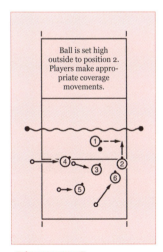
Diagram 17C

HOW TO PLAY THE GAME

Service reception formations

Service reception formations are designed to counteract the opponent's service, control the ball, and then proceed with the elements of the basic volleyball play. Players are placed on the court to optimize their abilities to control the ball and run an effective attack. It is important to understand the overlap rule in order to place players in correct rotational formations.

The overlap rule states that at time of service, each frontcourt player (positions 2, 3, and 4) must be closer to the centre line than his or her corresponding backcourt player (positions 1, 6, and 5 respectively). The player in position 3 must be between players in positions 2 and 4, and the player in position 6 must be between players in positions 1 and 5. The server is exempt from this rule. Once the ball has been served, players may move to any position in the playing area.

The four-on-four situation — Line service reception

The players in positions 2 and 4 respectively start on the right and left ends of the "line." The player in position 5 starts in the middle of a line that would join players in positions 2 and 4. The player in position 1 is the setter and starts behind the player in position 2. The setter is in effect "hidden" from handling the serve (Diagram 18A).

On contact of the ball by the server, the setter proceeds to the target area while teammates attempt to control the ball and execute the elements of the basic volleyball play. After the ball crosses the net, the players go to their initial defensive positions.

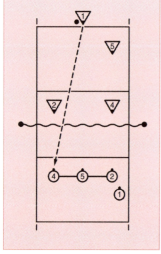

Diagram 18A

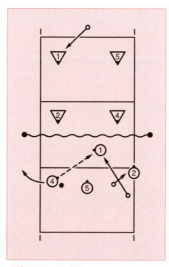

Diagram 18B

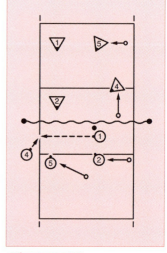

Diagram 18C

BASIC VOLLEYBALL CONCEPTS

The five-on-five situation — Cup service reception (fifth player in position 6; penetrating setter in position 1)

The players make a "cup" or semicircle formation with players in positions 2 and 4 respectively at the right and left sides of the "cup." Players in positions 5 and 6 are placed toward the middle of the court and nearer to the end line. The setter in position 1 "hides" behind the player in position 2 (Diagram 19A).

On contact of the ball by the server, the setter proceeds to the target area while teammates attempt to control the ball and execute the elements of the basic volleyball play. After the ball crosses the net, the players go to their initial defensive positions. Note that the serving team is playing a 6-up defence and makes the appropriate defensive movements.

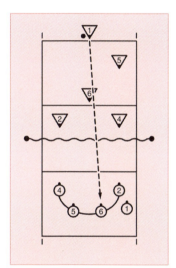

Diagram 19A

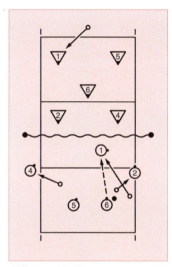

Diagram 19B

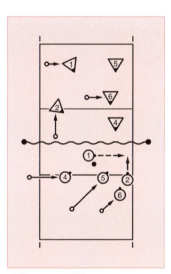

Diagram 19C

HOW TO PLAY THE GAME

The five-on-five situation — Cup service reception
(fifth player in position 6; nonpenetrating setter in position 2)

The players make a "cup" or semicircle formation with players in positions 1 and 4 respectively at the right and left sides of the "cup." Players in positions 5 and 6 are placed toward the middle of the court and nearer to the end line. The setter in position 2 "hides" at the net, thus hidden from handling the serve (Diagram 20A).

On contact of the ball by the server, the setter is at the target area while teammates attempt to control the ball and execute the elements of the basic volleyball play. In this situation, the only setting option is to set the ball high outside to the left sideline of the court (position 4). After the ball crosses the net, the players go to their initial defensive positions. Note that the serving team is playing a 6-back defence and makes the appropriate defensive movements.

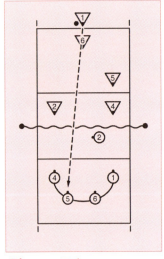
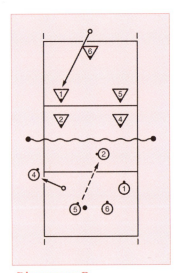
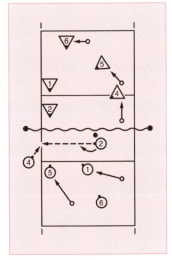

Diagram 20A   *Diagram 20B*   *Diagram 20C*

BASIC VOLLEYBALL CONCEPTS

The five-on-five situation — Cup service reception
(fifth player in position 3; penetrating setter in position 1)

The players make a "cup" or semicircle formation with players in positions 2 and 4 respectively at the right and left sides of the "cup." Players in positions 3 and 5 are placed toward the middle of the court and nearer to the end line. The player in position 3 is closer to the left sideline of the court. Placement of this player minimizes movement and potential confusion after the ball has been passed. The setter in position 1 "hides" behind the player in position 2 (Diagram 21A).

On contact of the ball by the server, the setter proceeds to the target area while teammates attempt to control the ball and execute the elements of the basic volleyball play. Attackers go to their attack ready positions after the ball has been passed. The serving team is playing with the fifth player in position 3 and makes the appropriate defensive movements. After the ball crosses the net, the players go to their initial defensive positions.

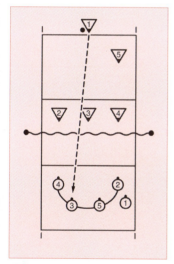

Diagram 21A

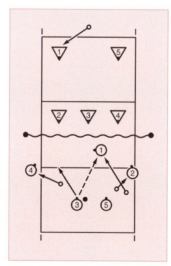

Diagram 21B

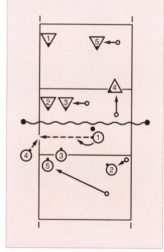

Diagram 21C

HOW TO PLAY THE GAME

The five-on-five situation — Cup service reception
(fifth player in position 3; nonpenetrating setter in position 2)

The players make a "cup" or semicircle formation with players in positions 1 and 4 respectively at the right and left sides of the "cup." Players in positions 3 and 5 are placed toward the middle of the court and nearer to the end line. The player in position 3 is closer to the left side of the court. Placement of this player minimizes movement and potential confusion after the ball has been passed. The setter in position 2 "hides" at the net, thus hidden from handling the serve (Diagram 22A).

On contact of the ball by the server, the setter is at the target area while teammates attempt to control the ball and execute the elements of the basic volleyball play. With a middle attacking situation, the first pass to the net should be directed slightly to the right of the middle. Note that attackers go to their attack ready positions after the ball has been passed. The serving team is playing with the fifth player in position 3 and makes the appropriate defensive movements. After the ball crosses the net, the players go to their initial defensive positions.

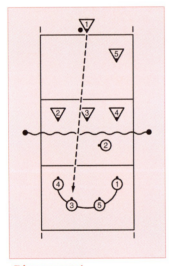

Diagram 22A

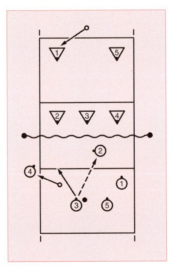

Diagram 22B

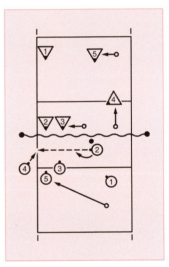

Diagram 22C

BASIC VOLLEYBALL CONCEPTS

The five-on-five situation — Line service reception
(fifth player in position 3; nonpenetrating setter in position 2)

Having the player in position 3 in the service reception formation may take away from a team's attack effectiveness, especially if the goal is to run a quick middle attack. To maximize attack effectiveness, the player in position 3 is taken out of service reception by "hiding" at the net. With two players (middle attacker in position 3 and the setter in position 2) being "hidden" from service reception, the formation reverts to a line formation (Diagram 23A). Note that after contact of the ball by the server, the player in position 3 goes to the middle attacker ready position to prepare for the attack.

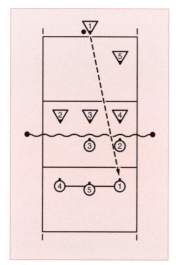

Diagram 23A

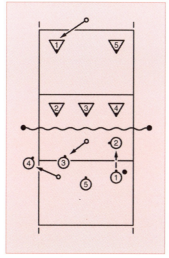

Diagram 23B

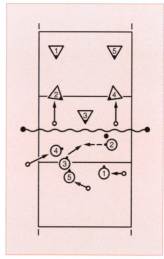

Diagram 23C

HOW TO PLAY THE GAME

The five-on-five situation — Line service reception (fifth player in position 3; penetrating setter in position 1)

The players make a line formation with players in positions 2 and 4 respectively on the right and left ends of the line. The player in position 5 starts in the middle of the line that would join players in positions 2 and 4. The player in position 1 is the setter and starts behind the player in position 2. The player in position 3 starts at the net in the middle. The setter and middle attacker are in effect "hidden" from handling the serve (Diagram 24A).

On contact of the ball by the server, the setter proceeds to the target area, the middle attacker proceeds to the middle attacker ready position, while teammates attempt to control the ball and execute the elements of the basic volleyball play. In the diagram, the ball is set to the player in position 2. The serving team makes the appropriate defensive movements. After the ball crosses the net, the players on the receiving team go to their initial defensive positions.

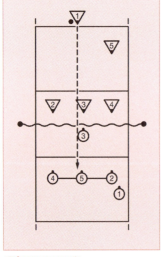

Diagram 24A

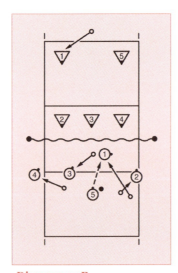

Diagram 24B

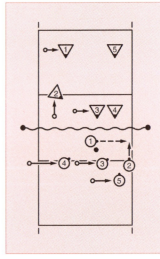

Diagram 24C

BASIC VOLLEYBALL CONCEPTS

The six-on-six situation

A multitude of service reception formations can be employed in the six-on-six situation. The simplest is the W formation and can be used in both nonpenetrating and penetrating setter situations. Cup formations are utilized to "hide" weak passers or to get hitters in optimal positions on the court to attack. Most elite teams use variations of line, or three-person, service reception patterns. Not only does the line formation "hide" weak passers and get hitters into optimal attacking positions, but it also minimizes interactions that may lead to confusion with regard to who should be playing the ball. Foundations of cup and line service reception formations have already been outlined in the four-on-four and five-on-five situations.

W service reception

A simple step-by-step approach to place players in the proper W service reception formation follows (also see Diagram 25A–F):

Step-by-step approach to W service reception

1. Draw a "W" on the court, with the top of the "W" closest to the net.
2. Frontcourt players move to the top of the "W."
3. Hide the setter.
4. Place hitters in optimal position to attack.
5. Fill in the remainder of the "W" with minimal movement and respecting the overlap rule.

HOW TO PLAY THE GAME

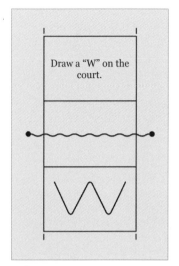

Diagram 25A

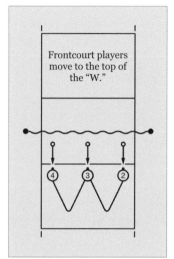

Diagram 25B

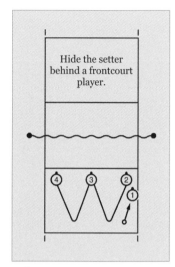

Diagram 25C

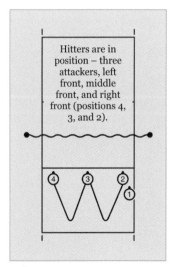

Diagram 25D

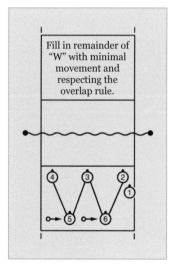

Diagram 25E

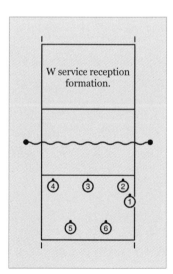

Diagram 25F

BASIC VOLLEYBALL CONCEPTS

Other W service reception formations

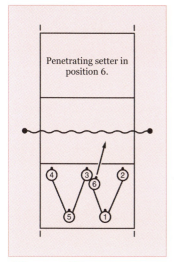

Diagram 26A

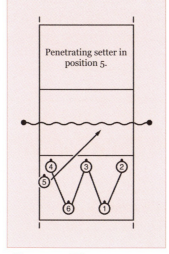

Diagram 26B

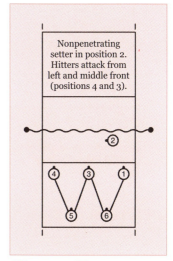

Diagram 26C

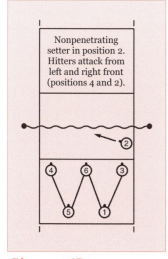

Diagram 26D

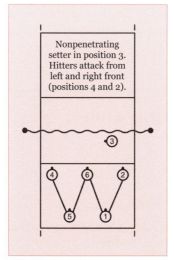

Diagram 26E

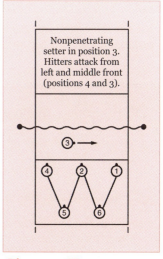

Diagram 26F

69

HOW TO PLAY THE GAME

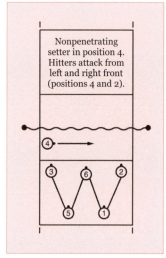

Diagram 26G

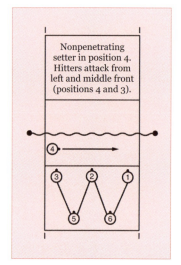

Diagram 26H

Cup service reception formations

Cup, or four-person, service reception formations are utilized for a number of reasons. They are primarily used to better position hitters for the attack or to hide a weak passer. Numerous variations can be used. A simple step-by-step approach to place players in the proper cup service reception formation follows (also see Diagram 27A–C):

Step-by-step approach to cup service reception

1. Frontcourt players move to the top of the "W."
2. Hide setter, weak passer, or hitter to be better positioned.
3. Place hitters in appropriate positions.
4. Fill in the remainder of the "cup" with minimal movement and respecting the overlap rule.

BASIC VOLLEYBALL CONCEPTS

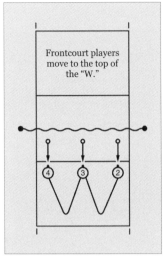

Diagram 27A

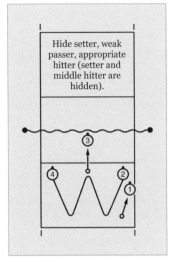

Diagram 27B

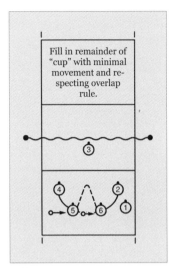

Diagram 27C

Examples of various cup service reception formations

Penetrating setter

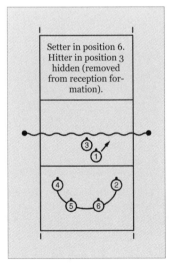

Diagram 28A

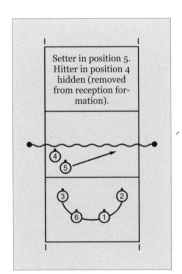

Diagram 28B

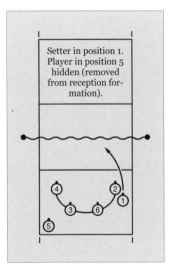

Diagram 28C

HOW TO PLAY THE GAME

Nonpenetrating setter

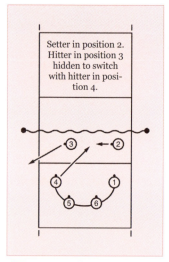

Setter in position 2. Hitter in position 3 hidden to switch with hitter in position 4.	Setter in position 4. Hitter in position 2 hidden to be able to attack middle.	

Diagram 29A

Diagram 29B

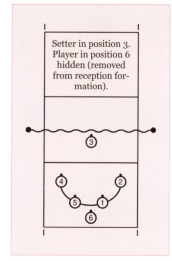

Setter in position 3. Player in position 6 hidden (removed from reception formation).

Diagram 29C

Coaches utilize various service reception formations to maximize the ability levels of the players.

BASIC VOLLEYBALL CONCEPTS

Team play worksheet

Coaches may use the following worksheet to set up their own individual service reception formations, attack patterns, and defensive alignments.

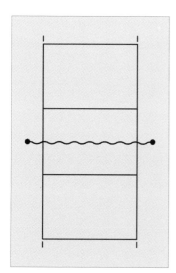
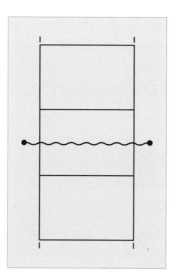
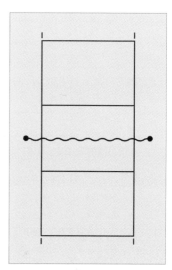
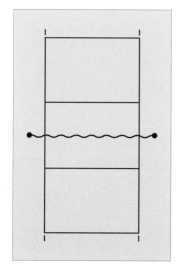
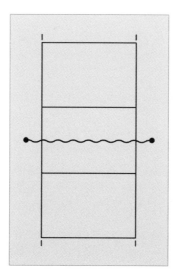
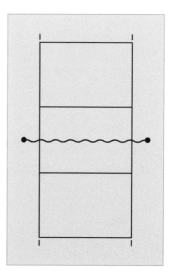

PART IV

DEVELOPING TECHNICAL SKILLS WITHOUT THE BALL 76
    Movement 76
    Agility 78
    Jumping 82

DEVELOPING TECHNICAL SKILLS WITH THE BALL 84
    Getting used to the ball 84
    Serving 86
    Passing and receiving 89
    Attacking 94

DEVELOPING TECHNICAL AND TACTICAL SKILLS WITH AN OPPONENT 98
    Serving and receiving 98
    Complex passing 102
    Attack defence 105

DEVELOPING ADVANCED PLAYING ABILITY 108
    Mini-games 108
    Games with opponents of unequal numbers 112

LEAD-UP GAMES

This section includes a collection of lead-up games that have either a direct or an indirect relationship to playing volleyball effectively. Lead-up games are an important part of volleyball practices, as they are enjoyable in themselves and have performance-stimulating characteristics. They provide a connecting link between basic preparation and volleyball-specific training because they can be used to prepare, develop, and strengthen players' technical and tactical abilities. As part of modern volleyball training, they should be used in ways that are well balanced with other aspects of training.

Each lead-up game can fulfill certain functions with respect to physical, technical, tactical, or psychological development. In order for these lead-up games to be most effective, they should have a specific purpose and meet the objectives the coach has set for the practice. The following tips should be considered:

- Use lead-up games mainly as an introduction for new movements and techniques of the game. They can also serve as a refresher during the middle part of training and provide some counterbalance to the more demanding volleyball-specific drills and training elements. Lead-up games can be used as fun drills to end practices and workouts in an upbeat manner.

- Lead-up games should follow a progression, moving from simple to more complex. It is important to build on previous experiences by developing a progression of lead-up games for each skill taught.

- Know the game very well. Small organizational mistakes confuse the players and lower the value of practice. Well-planned lead-up games make practice enjoyable and increase players' motivation for further improvements.

- Explain the lead-up games clearly and demonstrate before the players practice them. The explanation should be clear and concise, making sure that every player has a clear understanding of the task.

- Equipment has to be ready to ensure a quick start of the game. This also applies to team markings, floor markings, etc.

- Make sure that the lead-up games are executed correctly. After a clear explanation and demonstration, it is the coach's responsibility to see that the lead-up game is performed correctly. If the execution is sloppy or not correct, the practice must be stopped and the correct method emphasized one more time.

- As much as possible, introduce competition into lead-up games. This raises the intensity level of practice. Acknowledge the winner and praise good work.

- Check whether everything was done to give the selected lead-up game an aspect of enjoyment.

LEAD-UP GAMES

Developing technical skills without the ball

Movement

Coaching note

Movement efficiency provides the building blocks for successful skill execution. The development of a broad range of movement skills increases athletes' abilities to get into optimal court position to make the next play. The more stable and balanced athletes are when executing a skill, the more consistent their skill executions will be.

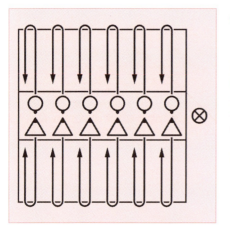

G1 End line race Two groups of equal number stand facing each other in the centre of the playing area. When the signal is given, both groups turn and run to the end line behind them and back. The first group to return to its original position receives a point. Starting positions (e.g., standing, sitting, lying face down, etc.) and mode of movement (e.g., running, skipping, hopping, etc.) can be varied. The team with the most points after several rounds is the winner.

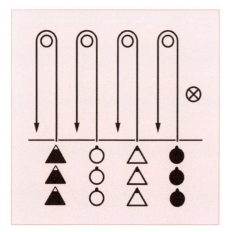

G2 Relay competition Several groups of equal number line up in a row behind a designated start line with adequate separation between groups. Each group has a marker (e.g., a cone or pylon) positioned several metres ahead of it. At the signal, the first member of each group runs up to and around the marker, returns to the start line, and tags the next player in line, and so on. The first group to return to its original position wins. If numbers are uneven to start, one player can go twice. *Variation*: Players complete the relay using various modes of movement, such as seal walk, crab walk, ball between the legs, etc.

WITHOUT THE BALL

G3 **Start tag** The players and one player chosen to be IT stand on opposite sides of a playing area divided into three equal parts. At the signal, all players try to successfully make it from one end line to the other without being tagged by IT. Before tagging any players, IT must first run across a third of the playing area to pick up an object, such as a cone, to be used to tag other players. In subsequent rounds, all players who have been tagged must also pick up cones and help IT tag other players. The winner is the last player tagged.

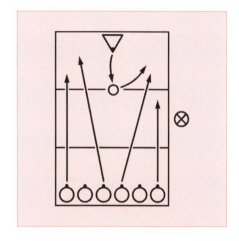

G4 **Black and white** Two teams of equal number lie on their backs, soles of their feet touching in the centre of the playing area. One team is called "black" and the other is called "white." At the coach's signal ("black" or "white"), members of that team must run to the end line behind them as members of the opposing team pursue them. The goal of the other team is to tag as many players as possible before they reach the end line safely. The team gets a point for each opposing player tagged. After repeating the game several times, the team tallying the most points is the winner.

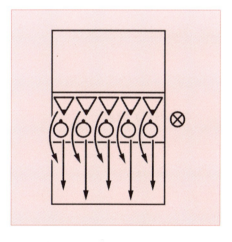

G5 **Position change** Two teams of equal number stand facing each other at opposite ends of a rectangular playing area. At the signal, both teams run to opposite sides. The first team to stand in a row along the opposite end line wins.

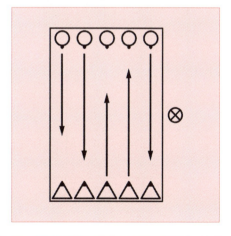

LEAD-UP GAMES

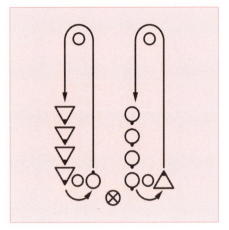

G6 **Chase** Two teams position themselves as shown. Each team assigns one player to the other team, who becomes IT. At the signal, players begin running around a pylon in the same direction, and IT must try to tag the last player on the opposing team. Each team tries to prevent this as long as possible without losing their original order. The first team to successfully tag a player gains a point. New players are chosen to be IT for each round.

Agility

Coaching note

Agility is considered the most prominent factor in general athletic ability. It is the ability to change direction of the body and its parts rapidly. Actions in volleyball are short and quick, requiring high levels of agility.

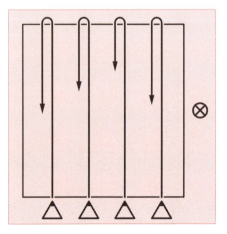

G7 **Save your soul** Players stand behind one end line of a rectangular playing area. At the signal, all players run to the opposite end line and back. The last player to return to the starting end line after each round receives a point and starts 1 metre ahead of everyone else in the next round. The objective is to finish the game with as few points as possible.

WITHOUT THE BALL

G8 Accordion run A rectangular playing area is divided into three equal parts marked by lines. Players start at one end line and have to run to each line and back (i.e., to the first line and back, to the second line and back, and to the final line and back). This requires fast running and turning. The winner is the player with the most wins after several rounds.

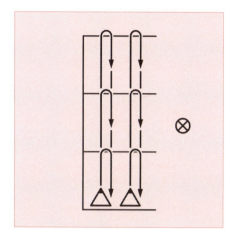

G9 Row run Teams of equal number stand in rows next to each other. All players are given a number. When the coach calls out a number, the player from each team with that number must run around his team in a counterclockwise direction before returning to his original position. The first player to return to his original position receives a point for the team. Different numbers are called out in each round until all players have run at least once. The team accumulating the most points wins.

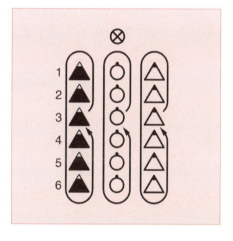

G10 Circle tag A small group (not more than 10 players) stands in a circle formation holding hands. A player chosen to be IT stands outside the circle and must try to tag a designated player from the circle. The circle tries to protect this player from being tagged by turning, but must do so without breaking the circle (i.e., releasing hands). When the player is successfully tagged, a different player becomes IT.

LEAD-UP GAMES

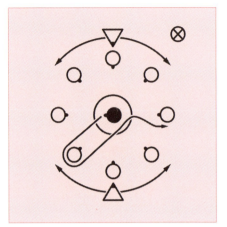

G11 Circling One group (not larger than 12 to 15 players) stands in a circle. One player stands in the middle of the circle and two others stand outside the circle. At the signal, the player in the middle tries to circle around one member of the circle without being tagged by one of the two players outside the circle. The player inside the circle must try to circle three different players. If the runner gets tagged, the tagger becomes a runner, or three new people are chosen.

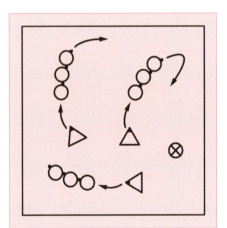

G12 Attaching In groups of three, each player stands holding the hips of the player in front of her (except the first player). One group of three is IT. Individually, the players who are IT try to get themselves attached to a group by grabbing the hips of the last player in line. The group tries to avoid this by turning. If a player manages to become attached, her team is no longer IT – the team that has been captured becomes the IT team.

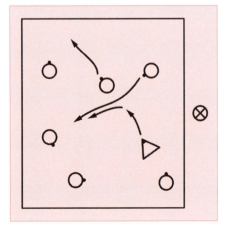

G13 Cross tag A pursued player can be saved if another player runs between this player and IT, thus cutting the path between IT and the player. IT then is not allowed to continue pursuing the original player. However, he may attempt to tag the person crossing his path. If IT is successful, roles are reversed.

WITHOUT THE BALL

G14 **Chain tag** One or more players are IT to begin the game. As players are tagged, they must join hands with IT, becoming part of a longer chain. The chain must remain connected at all times, so only the first and last players forming the chain are able to tag remaining players. The game continues until all players have been tagged.

G15 **Tag the third** Players are paired (linked by the arms) and scattered throughout the playing area. Two players remain unpaired, one of whom begins the game as IT. IT tries to tag the other unpaired player, who can save herself by linking arms with one of the pairs. Only two players can be linked at one time, so when a third player links up with a pair, the outermost player must release and form a new pair while avoiding being tagged, and so on. If IT successfully tags another player before she is able to link up with another pair, that player becomes IT. No touchbacks are allowed.

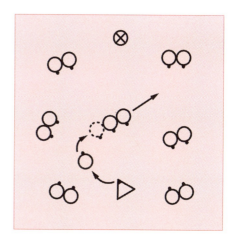

G16 **Relay tag** A group of players is chosen to be IT and sits or stands along the end line of a square playing area. Another group of equal number moves around within the playing area. One at a time, each player who is IT has to run into the playing area and tag one player before being able to run back outside the playing area. When a player is successfully tagged and IT has left the playing area, the next player who is IT enters the playing area, must tag another player, and so on. The game is over when each tagger has tagged one player. Roles are later reversed.

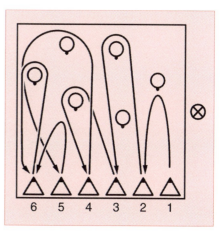

LEAD-UP GAMES

Jumping

Coaching note

Jumping is one of the most important elements in the game of volleyball. Net play involving attacking and blocking obviously requires jumping, but actions such as jump setting and diving for balls are also enhanced by the ability to jump. A shorter athlete's ability to jump can more than compensate for a lack of size.

G17 Jumping over a distance Players line up in a row behind a designated start line. At the signal, players have to cover a specified distance by jumping. The coach or instructor will determine whether it is left-footed, right-footed, or two-footed jumping, as well as how many times the players will be required to jump the specified distance.

G18 Grid jump fight Players stand in pairs facing each other on one foot with arms crossed. One player stands in a small grid, marked by four cones, while the other jumps around the outside. Both have their arms crossed and try to get the other player to put both feet down. The player outside the grid also tries to push the other one outside the grid. Players switch positions after each round. The player winning the most rounds is the winner. *Variation*: Arms must remain behind the back with one hand holding the other arm by the elbow. One foot is held behind the back by the free hand.

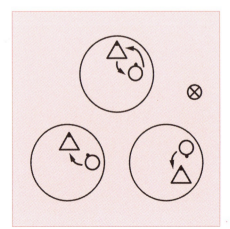

G19 Rooster fight Two players face each other in a fighting position (arms crossed in front, standing on one leg) and jump toward each other when the signal is given. Players try knocking each other off balance without unfolding their arms, until one player is forced to put both feet on the ground. The game can be played in teams – the winning team would be the one with the most players still on one leg with arms crossed after a specified period of time. A circular fighting ring may also be used to make the game more difficult. Any player stepping out of the ring would be eliminated.

WITHOUT THE BALL

G20 **Jump tag** Two groups stand facing each other a few metres apart at one end of the playing area. One group is IT to start the game. At the signal, the players must begin jumping toward a goal line at the opposite end of the playing area. Players who are IT must try tagging as many of them as possible (also while jumping) before they safely reach the goal. Groups switch roles after each round. Points are tallied after a few rounds to determine the winner.

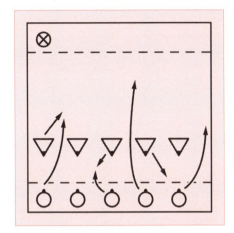

G21 **Jumping over players** Two groups each form a circle lying face down with their heads toward the centre. At the signal, the first player in each group gets up and jumps over the other players in a counterclockwise direction until returning to his original position. As soon as the first player has jumped over the person next to him, this player also gets up and begins jumping over the others in the same direction, and so on, until each player has jumped over every other player. The first team to have each member return to his original position is the winner.

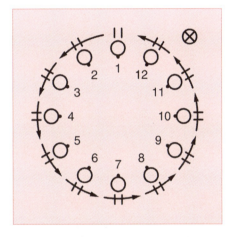

G22 **Jumping over the rope** The coach or another player stands in the middle of a circle formed by the remaining players. The player in the middle swings a rope with a ball (or similar object) attached to the end of it just above the ground in a clockwise direction, for 5 to 10 revolutions. Players in the circle must jump over the rope as it passes them. If a player touches the rope at any time, she replaces the player in the middle; otherwise, players take turns as the middle player. *Variations*: (a) Speed and height of the swing can be varied; (b) players move and jump in the opposite direction of the swing.

LEAD-UP GAMES

Developing technical skills with the ball

Getting used to the ball

Coaching note

Ball control is fundamental to success in the game of volleyball. Having athletes contact the ball in a variety of non-volleyball-specific situations will only increase their ability to effectively handle the ball when playing in volleyball matches.

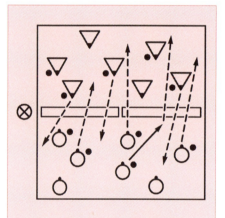

G23 **Balls be gone** Two teams stand facing each other on opposite sides of a playing area divided equally by a row of benches. Each team starts with the same number of balls. At the signal, each team tries to get its balls into the opponent's half of the playing area as fast as possible. The balls can be thrown, kicked, or moved by any other means. The game is played for a specified time, or until all the balls are in one half of the playing area at one time. If playing for a limited time, the team with the fewest balls in its half wins. *Variation*: The game is played on a volleyball court divided by a net.

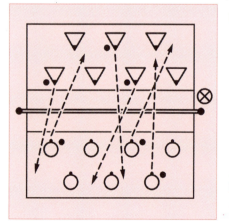

G24 **Multi-ball** Two teams stand facing each other on opposite sides of a playing area divided equally by a net or rope. The objective is to get as many balls as possible into the opposing team's half without having them caught or go out of bounds. Any technique can be used to get the balls over the net. Players cannot cross a line 1 metre away from the net on each side when passing the ball over. Any player crossing this line loses a point for the team. Balls can be passed among team members as often as desired. *Variation*: Players must pass a ball over to the other side immediately upon receiving it.

WITH THE BALL

G25 Ball retrieval race Two teams stand facing each other at opposite ends of a playing area, with several balls placed along the centre line. At the signal, both teams run to retrieve as many balls as possible and bring them back to their starting lines (one at a time). The team gathering the most balls is the winner. *Variation*: The coach chooses a progression of skills: set 1 – volleying the ball above the head continuously back to the starting line; set 2 – bumping the ball continuously back to the starting line; set 3 – alternating between volleying and bumping the ball back to the starting line. If a ball is dropped, it is returned to the centre line.

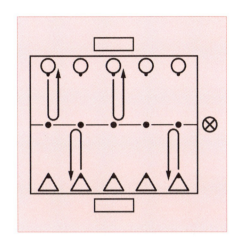

G26 Goal ball Players are divided into two equal teams. Players on one team are each given a ball and stand around a basketball hoop. At the signal, the players try to make as many baskets as possible by volleying the ball into the hoop within a given time (20 to 60 seconds). The teams then switch, and the drill is repeated for the other team. The team that makes the most baskets in the allotted time is the winner. *Variations*: (a) Players use the forearm pass; (b) teams compete at separate hoops simultaneously; (c) same as (b), but the first team to a given number wins; (d) players must stand outside the key area to score.

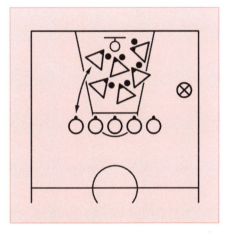

G27 Ball toss Players are each given a ball and divided into two equal teams. Each team stands on opposite sides of a playing area or volleyball court divided into two equal halves. Members of each team distribute themselves along both end lines. At the signal, players on both teams try tossing their balls into a basket located in the centre of each half of the playing area. The ball must remain in the basket to count as a point. When all players have attempted a shot, players retrieve their own balls. The team making the most baskets after several rounds is the winner. *Variation*: The balls must be volleyed or bumped into the basket.

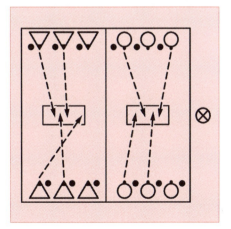

LEAD-UP GAMES

Serving

Coaching note

The serve is obviously an integral aspect of a volleyball match. Too often its importance is underestimated. Not only does the serve initiate a rally, but it is also a team's first chance at offence. A highly effective serve can minimize the effectiveness of the opponent's offence or even score an outright winner – an ace.

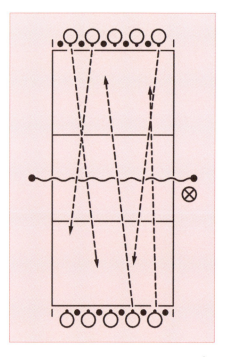

G28 **End line serving** Two teams of equal number stand facing each other on opposite end lines of the volleyball court. Each player is given a ball to start. At the signal, all players from both teams try to serve as many balls as possible into the opposing team's half of the court continuously for a specified period of time. The winner is the team with the most successful serves in the allotted time. The coach, manager, or a player from each team should be assigned to keep score for one team in each round. *Variation*: Serving errors are subtracted from the team's total score.

WITH THE BALL

G29 **Series serve** Two groups of equal number position themselves behind opposite end lines of a volleyball court. All players line up behind the end line with a ball. Starting with the first player, each team serves until it has reached a specified number of consecutive serves. The team calls out each successful serve. Each successful series (going through the entire team once) earns 1 point. The winner is determined after several rounds of play. *Variation*: Players from each team alternate serving. If a serve is missed, all players from that team line up and sprint from the end line to the attack line, back to the end line, to the centre line, and finally back to the end line.

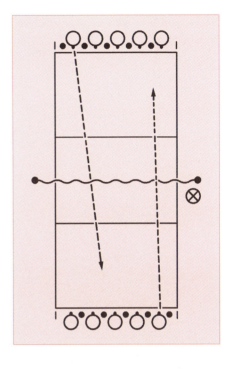

G30 **Serve and follow** Players are each given a ball and distribute themselves evenly behind the end lines of a volleyball court. At the signal, one player on each side of the court serves the ball to a target person positioned on the right side of the court (position 5). The server follows the ball and becomes the next target. The target retrieves the ball and joins the end of the serving line at the end of the court. The next player to serve should wait until the target player has moved into position before serving the ball. This pattern of serve-and-follow continues until each player has successfully completed a certain number of serves. *Variations*: (a) A target player stands at various positions on the court; (b) after serving, players move to a designated waiting area outside the sideline of the court, and the player in the waiting area becomes the next target.

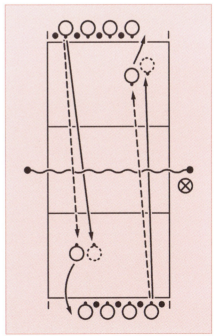

LEAD-UP GAMES

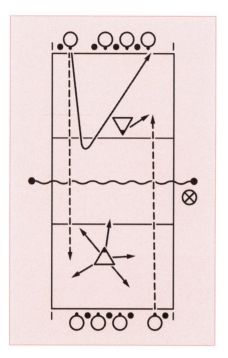

G31 **Serve and catch** On a volleyball court, two teams alternate serving behind opposite end lines. One player from each team, positioned in the middle of the court on each side of the net, must try catching the serves of the opposing team. If a ball touches the floor or is dropped, the catcher and server switch positions. The player who remains "catcher" longest is the winner. *Variations*: (a) After serving the ball, players must run into the court past their own attack line before rejoining the serving line; (b) teams alternate serving. After a player serves, he becomes the next catcher. Points are awarded as follows: the serving team scores 2 points if the ball lands on the court without being touched and 1 point if it is touched but not caught; the receiving team scores 2 points if there is a service error and 1 point if the ball is caught. The game is played to 25 points and a team must win by 2 points.

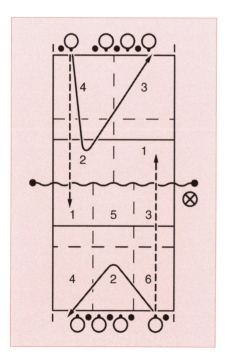

G32 **Golf** Two teams of equal number stand facing each other behind opposite end lines of a volleyball court. One at a time, players try to serve the ball into one of four (easy course) or six (difficult course) marked sections on the court. Each team has a designated serving order, and serving players must run into a designated section after each ball is served. The drill continues until all players have successfully served one ball in each of the marked sections or until one team has successfully served at least one ball in each section. *Variation*: The marked sections are designated as holes with a specific order being followed. A ball must be served into the hole before the hole is completed and the team can move on to the next hole. Each serve counts as a stroke. Each service error counts as a stroke penalty. The team with the fewest strokes is the winner.

WITH THE BALL

Passing and receiving

> **Coaching note**
>
> *Without mastering passing and receiving, volleyball cannot be played well at any level. Passing and receiving are done instantaneously in that the ball cannot be caught but must rebound off the arms or cupped hands. Cooperative, rather than competitive, lead-up games can best be used to develop passing and receiving skills.*

G33 High ball A rectangular playing area (or volleyball court) is divided in half lengthwise with four teams positioned on opposite sides as shown in the diagram. The goal is to pass the ball over a net (or rope) without letting the ball hit the ground or go out of bounds. The team that successfully passes the ball longest is the winner. *Variations*: (a) The game can also be played without a net. In this case, the goal is to pass the ball beyond a designated line on each side of the playing area; (b) a maximum of three touches are permitted per side before the ball must be sent back over to the other side; (c) the ball is played diagonally across the net.

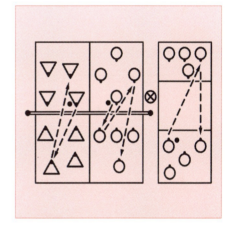

G34 Partner feed Players are divided into pairs and line up facing each other from a given distance. One player feeds the ball to the other 10 times, and the ball is played (volleyed or bumped) back to the feeder. After 10 successful passes, roles are reversed. The winner of each round is the player who makes the fewest errors. *Variations*: (a) The feeding partner must call out which skill to use ("volley" or "bump"); (b) the ball is played to a partner on the opposite side of a net or rope; (c) one player volleys the ball and the partner bumps it back, trying to achieve a given number of consecutive contacts.

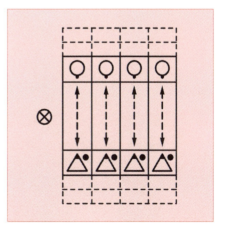

LEAD-UP GAMES

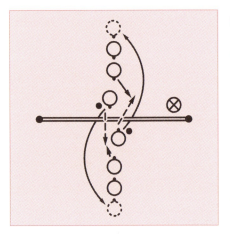

G35 **Shuttle passing** Two teams stand in a row facing each other on opposite sides of a net or rope. The first player on one team begins by passing the ball over the net to the first player on the other team. After playing the ball over, each player must run under the net to join the end of the row on the other side. The drill continues until someone commits an error, which results in a point for that player. Errors include not getting the ball over the net, passing the ball out of bounds, or allowing the ball to touch the floor. Players receiving 3 points are out of the game. The last remaining player wins. *Variation*: Two balls are played simultaneously as shown.

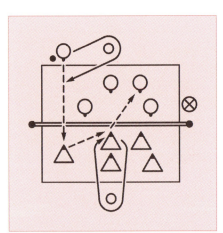

G36 **Volleyball tennis** Two teams stand on opposite sides of a net or rope. The ball is played back and forth, and can only bounce once before being played to a teammate or back over the net. The first team to reach 15 points wins the set. An error results in a point when the ball touches the net, goes out of bounds, bounces more than once, or is played more than three times by one team. Players rotate one position clockwise after each point, and the ball goes to the team that lost the previous point. *Variation*: After each successful pass over the net, players must run around a cone behind the end line before rejoining the play.

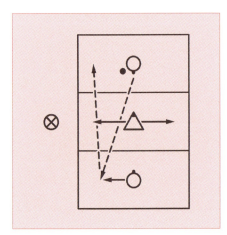

G37 **Monkey in the middle** A playing area is divided into three equal sections, with one player occupying each section. The two outermost players pass the ball to each other continuously, trying to keep it out of the reach of the player in the middle (the monkey), while also keeping it within the boundaries of the playing area. After a passing error (the ball does not land in the correct section of the playing area or the ball is intercepted by the monkey), the player who committed the error becomes the new monkey. The winner is the player with the least number of errors after a given amount of time.

WITH THE BALL

G38 **Ball at the wall** Players are divided into two or more equal groups. A series of lines are drawn parallel to a large, smooth wall at various distances from the wall. Each team lines up in a row (one behind the other) facing the wall behind the first line. Each player volleys (or bumps) the ball against the wall so it rebounds back past the start line with one bounce. For each successful pass, the team receives a point. After each player has gone once, the starting distance from the wall is increased. The team with the most points after a certain number of rounds is the winner. *Variation*: The ball must be passed without a bounce.

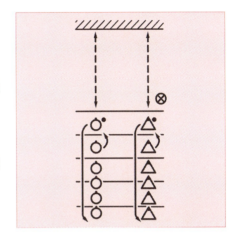

G39 **Exchange ball** Two or more groups position themselves in a triangular formation as shown in the diagram. One player is given a ball and begins the game as the passer from the top of the triangle. The passer passes to teammates one at a time from left to right, receiving a return pass after each pass, until every player has received a pass. Once the last player in line has made the final pass, she takes over as the passer, and the passer joins the other end of the row. The game continues until each player has been the passer once. The first team to have all players back in their original positions is the winner.

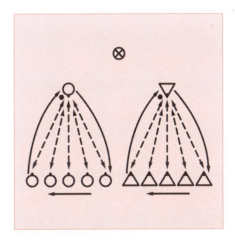

G40 **Pass over** Players are divided into two or more equal teams. Teams are then divided in half, each half lining up (single file) facing the other from a given distance behind two lines or benches. The first player from each team is given a ball. He passes (volleys or bumps) to the first player across from him and then moves to the end of the line, and so on. The winner is the first team to successfully complete a specified number of passes. *Variation*: A net can be used to divide the playing area instead of benches.

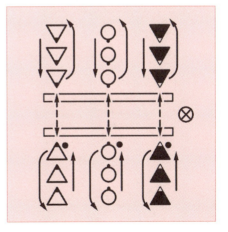

LEAD-UP GAMES

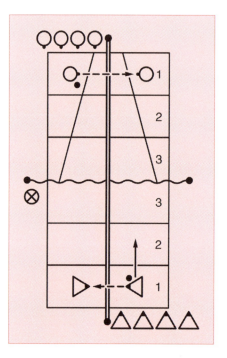

G41 Three-section series Two teams pair off and position themselves on opposite sides of a volleyball court as shown. The first pair on each side begins in the first section of the court near the end line. The goal for each pair is to complete a series of contacts (e.g., 20 consecutive volleys) over a net or rope before moving on to the second section, and so on. If unsuccessful, the pair moves to the back of the line and the next pair in line moves on to the court. Pairs that have successfully completed the series in all sections must wait until all other pairs have finished. The team that completes the series in each section in the fastest time is the winner. *Variations*: (a) Pairs must complete a different series of passes in each section (e.g., just volleys, just bumps, alternating volleys and bumps, etc.); (b) the distance between partners is increased as players move to new sections.

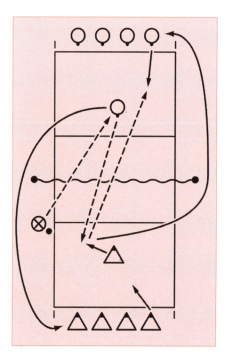

G42 Vollis Two groups stand along the end line of a volleyball court with one player from each team on the court. The coach tosses a ball to one side of the court, and the player must forearm pass the ball over the net and run to join the end of the opposite court (only one contact per side is allowed). The player on the opposite side forearm passes the ball back over the net as the next player on the first side enters the court. This pattern continues until the ball fails to cross the net or lands out of bounds. The person responsible for the error is out of the drill but must continuously jog around the playing area of the court. The coach always initiates the rally. *Variations*: (a) Two contacts are allowed before sending the ball over the net; (b) a player from the losing side forearm passes the ball over the net to initiate the rally; (c) players do not cross to the opposite side but stay on their own sides; (d) players play one-on-one until the rally ends, and sides score points for winning the rally.

WITH THE BALL

G43 **Ball over the net** This is a simple three-on-three "half-court" game intended for beginners. Two teams of three stand on opposite sides of the net. One team begins the game by serving from behind the attack line (3 metres away from the net). When the serve is received by a member of the opposing team, the ball must be played above the height of the net and caught by a teammate. The player who catches the ball then throws the ball up, catches it again (before it bounces), and plays the ball back over the net. The ball must be played by the same player twice before it is played over the net. Any mistakes (ball is not played above the height of the net, touches the net, hits the floor, goes out of bounds, or is not contacted by the same player twice) are counted as points for the opposing team. The team that scores the point begins the next rally with a serve.

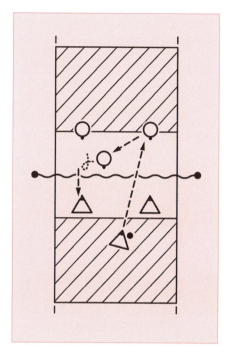

G44 **Winners** A team of two players starts on one side of a volleyball court designated as the "winner's" court. The other players are behind the end line of the "challenger's" court. A "challenger" team of two players begins the rally by serving from the end line. The winner of the rally goes to the "winner's" court, while the losers go behind the end line of the challenger's court. A new challenger team begins the next rally. Players or teams score points if they win a rally only when beginning on the winner's court. *Variations*: (a) Three contacts per side are made mandatory; b) any combination of players can be used – one-on-one, two-on-two, three-on-three, etc.

LEAD-UP GAMES

Attacking

Coaching note

Most athletes consider attacking to be the most exciting aspect of the game of volleyball. A good attacker not only hits the ball high and hard but also is able to subtly place the ball, thus making it difficult for an opponent to prevent the attack from scoring. The ability to control the body in the air while applying maximum power to the hit is essential for an effective attack.

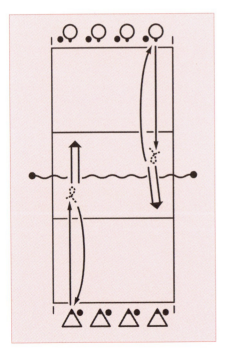

G45 **Net ball**   Players are divided into two equal teams and stand behind opposite end lines facing the net on a volleyball court. Each player is given a ball and, at the signal, one player at a time from each team must run up to the net, toss the ball to himself, and spike the ball over the net before returning to the starting position, when the next player begins. If there is an error with the spike, the player retrieves another ball from his own end line and continues until successful. The first team to have all its players back in line behind the end line is the winner.

WITH THE BALL

G46 **Box ball**   Two teams stand on opposite sides of boxes positioned in the middle of their side of a volleyball court. Each team is given three balls to start the game. Players must try to hit the box on the opposite side of the net with a spike from their respective sides of the net to receive a point for the team. Balls that miss the box and land in the opposing team's half of the court can be retrieved by the opposing team. The team with the highest score after a specified amount of time is the winner. *Variation*: 2 points are awarded for a successful hit if a teammate sets up the attack with a volley.

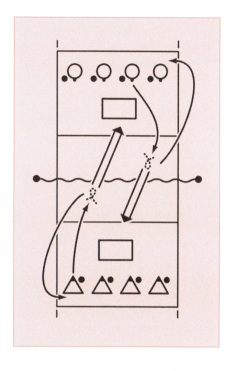

G47 **Wall duel**   A line is drawn a certain distance away from a large, smooth wall (depending on player abilities). Players are paired off and stand behind the line. One player starts the game by spiking the ball against the wall (the ball must hit the floor before it hits the wall), trying to make it difficult for the other player to catch the ball before it bounces again. Each player receives a point for every successful catch. The first player to reach a certain number of points is the winner. *Variation*: The ball must be continuously spiked against the wall (without catching), allowing one bounce between each hit.

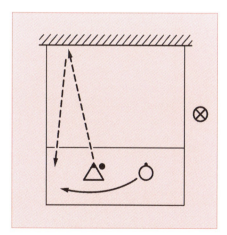

LEAD-UP GAMES

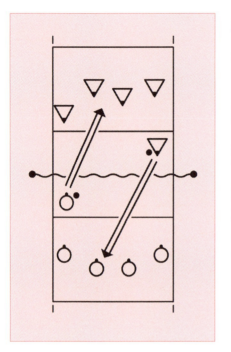

G48 **Avoid the middle** Two teams of equal number stand facing each other at opposite ends of a volleyball court. Teams can only spike from position 4 at the net. Balls cannot be spiked into the middle section (i.e., between the net and the attack line). Players repeatedly spike balls over to the other side, trying to prevent opposing players from successfully catching the ball. Points are awarded when the ball touches the floor in the opponent's section of the playing area, a ball is not caught successfully, or the ball goes out of bounds. After a certain amount of time has elapsed, the team with the most points wins. *Variation*: Each team must perform three contacts (i.e., bump, set, spike) when delivering the ball across to the other team.

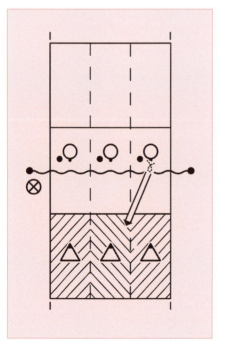

G49 **Pair spike at the net** Players are divided into pairs and face each other on opposite sides of a volleyball net. One player tosses the ball up to himself and, either from a standing position or with a three-step approach, spikes the ball over the net. The player on the other side of the net must try to catch the ball before it hits the floor. Each successful hit (the ball touches the floor in bounds) is worth 1 point. The players alternate attacking and defending. The game is over when one player reaches a certain number of points.

WITH THE BALL

G50 **Behind the attack line** Two evenly matched teams stand on opposite sides of a volleyball court. The ball is served from the attack line before each rally begins. All players must remain behind the attack line before each serve, the ball must be played from behind the attack line on each side, and the ball must be played to the other side beyond the attack line. The goal for each team is to spike the ball into the opposing team's court. Each team is allowed a maximum of three hits to get the ball over the net. If a player is not in a position to spike the ball, she may pass the ball over the net. Points are awarded when the ball touches the floor, the ball goes out of bounds, the ball bounces before the attack line, or a team fails to get the ball over the net with three contacts or fewer. The first team to reach a certain number of points wins. *Variation*: The coach tosses the ball at the attack line for a player to begin the rally with a spike.

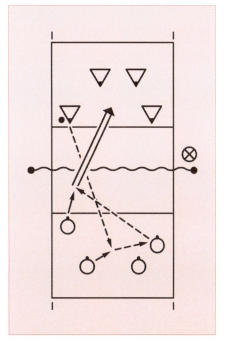

All players must have an awareness of the ball at all times during play.

LEAD-UP GAMES

Developing technical and tactical skills with an opponent

Serving and receiving

Coaching note

The first two contacts (serve and serve receive) in every rally can be critical in determining the eventual winner of a match. These elements should be worked on in every practice and should be worked on in a variety of competitive situations. All players should be able to perform these skills under pressure.

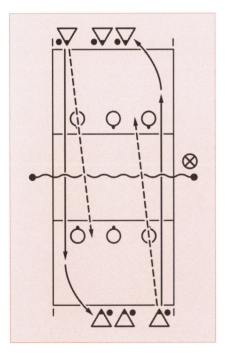

G51 **Serve and receive** Four groups of equal number set up on a volleyball court as shown. Two groups stand behind opposite end lines as servers, while the other two groups stand behind opposite attack lines as serve receivers. The first serving player serves, follows the ball, and joins the end of the serving line on the other side of the net. The players receiving the serves must try to (forearm) pass the ball so it lands between the attack line and the net on their side of the net. When the servers have returned to their original positions, players switch roles.

WITH AN OPPONENT

G52 Servers versus receivers Players are divided into two teams of six. Three players from each team are given a ball and alternate serving from behind the end line, while three players from each team receive the serves with either a forearm pass or a volley pass. Teams score points when the opposing team fails to keep the serve in bounds or when their passes do not land in bounds on their side of the net. When one team reaches 10 points, players switch positions (servers become receivers and vice versa). The first team to reach 20 points is the winner.

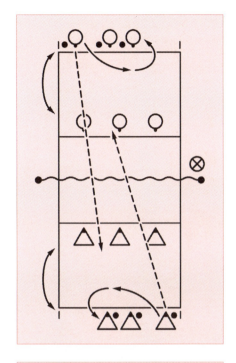

G53 Half-court serve and receive A volleyball court is divided in half lengthwise as shown. In each half, two groups of three stand facing each other on opposite sides of the net. Each member of one group of three is given a ball and stands behind the end line ready to serve. The other group has one player stand inside the court ready to receive the serve, while the other two players stand behind the end line. When the ball is served, the receiving player must (forearm) pass the ball above the height of the net and catch it before it lands (in bounds). Each player receives a point for successfully passing and catching the ball. Each player loses a point for making a service error. After each player of a group has served, roles are reversed. The player who accumulates the most points after a specified amount of time is the winner. *Variation*: Both players (server and receiver) move to opposite lines on opposite sides of the net after each sequence.

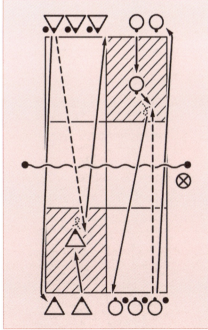

LEAD-UP GAMES

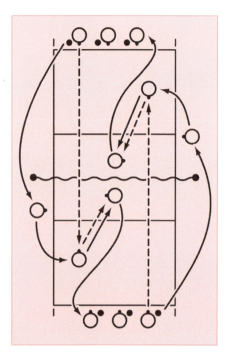

G54 Continuity serve and receive Players are set up on a volleyball court as shown. Servers are at the end lines of the court, targets are at the net, a passer is in position 5 on the court, and a floater waits on the sideline to become the next passer. One player serves the ball to the serve receiver, who attempts to pass the ball to the target. Players basically follow the ball. Servers go to the floater position, floaters become passers, and targets go the end line on the side they are on to become servers. Each player receives a point for successfully passing a ball. Each player loses a point for a service error. The player who accumulates the most points after a specified amount of time is the winner. *Variations*: (a) Receivers are in position 1; (b) target goes to the end line on the side the ball was served from (half-court continuity serve and receive).

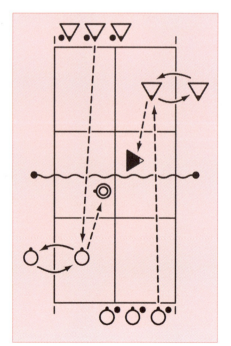

G55 Competition serve and receive A volleyball court is divided in half lengthwise as shown. On one half three players each have a ball and will alternate serving. Two players will alternate as serve receivers, and the third person will be a target at the net. Servers compete against each other and serve receivers compete against each other. Servers score a point when the receiver makes a poor pass or is aced. Servers lose a point if they make a service error. Receivers score a point when they make a perfect pass to the target. No points are scored with a poor pass, and a point is lost if the receiver is aced. The server and serve receiver who accumulate the most points after a specified amount of time are the respective winners.

WITH AN OPPONENT

G56 Three-player competition serve and receive Players are set up on a volleyball court as shown. There are three passers, a target, and a floater; the remaining players line up as servers on the end line of one side of the volleyball court. One player serves the ball at the passers. A passer attempts to pass the ball to the target. If the pass is a good pass, the passer counts a point and all players stay in their relative areas, with the server going to the end of the serving order. If the pass is poor, the passer becomes the target person, the floater fills in for the passer, the server becomes the floater, and the target goes to the serve area and is the last person in the serving order. The player who accumulates the most points after a specified amount of time is declared the winner. *Variation*: Play to a certain number of points.

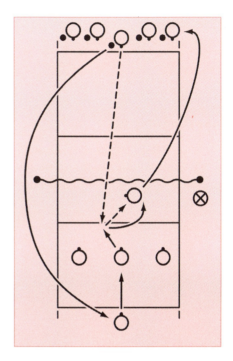

G57 Serve and receive elimination Two teams of equal number stand facing each other on opposite sides of a volleyball court as shown. Half of each team are servers (and stand behind the end line) and half are serve receivers (and stand within the court). The two teams alternate serving, trying to make their serves as difficult to handle as possible. The receiving team must (forearm) pass the ball above the height of the net and keep it in bounds on their side of the net. When a player makes two (or more) errors on the pass or the serve, he leaves the game. A passer is replaced by one of the servers on the team. When a team is down to six (or fewer) players, remaining team members alternate serving. The game continues for a specified period of time or until one team has no players left.

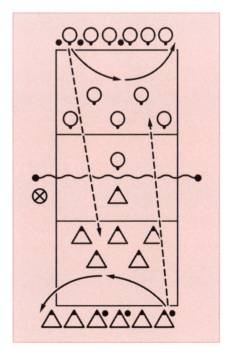

LEAD-UP GAMES

Complex passing

Coaching note

The game of volleyball is dynamic in nature. Passing skills should be practiced in dynamic situations. There can never be enough passing drills in a coach's repertoire. Teams that pass well are able to control the game.

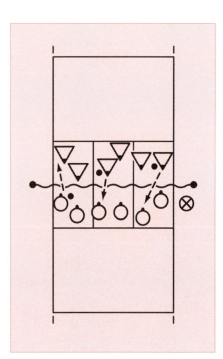

G58 Short court Players are divided into pairs and stand on opposite sides of a net in 3-metre by 3-metre playing areas. Each pair must play the ball back and forth (one contact) over a net until someone makes a mistake (the ball does not clear the net or goes out of bounds). A point is given to the opposing player for each mistake made. The player with the most points after a certain period of time is the winner. *Variations*: (a) Players must use a different skill for successive contacts (e.g., volley, bump, roll shot, bump, volley, etc.). In other words, players cannot use the same technique twice in a row for sending the ball back over the net; (b) play begins with a serve from the attack line, and a maximum of three contacts per side are allowed.

WITH AN OPPONENT

G59 **Forearm pass tennis** Two teams stand facing each other on opposite sides of a shortened volleyball court. The two teams alternate serving from behind the attack line. The serve must be received and played over the net with a forearm pass. Three contacts per side are allowed, as is blocking. If an error is made (the ball goes out of bounds, more than three hits are made, a contact other than a forearm pass is used – block excepted), the opposing team gets a point. Players rotate one position clockwise after each point. The first team to reach 25 points is the winner.

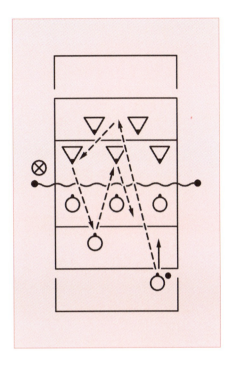

G60 **Pass, pass, and over** The volleyball court is divided into three equal areas lengthwise. Two players start in each area on either side of the net – one player at the net and the other between the attack line and the end line. One side serves the ball. The receiver passes the ball to his partner at the net and approaches the net to receive a return pass, which is sent over the net to the receiver on the other side of the net. The receiver and his partner, on the same side, then switch positions. This pattern continues until the ball is not controlled. This continues for either a given number of continuous contacts over the net or a given time period. *Variation*: Players put the ball over the net in order to win the rally.

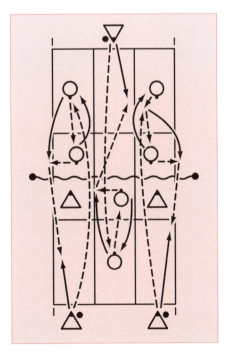

103

LEAD-UP GAMES

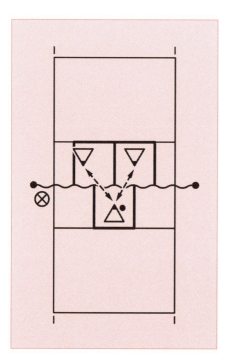

G61 Triangle passing game Three small square playing areas of equal size are marked on either side of a volleyball net as shown. One player stands in each playing area, so there are always two players on one side of the net facing one player on the other side. One player begins the game by playing the ball over the net to an opposing player, who must play the ball back over the net, and so on. Only one touch is allowed to get the ball over the net, and the ball must be played within the boundaries. When a player commits an error or the ball lands in his playing area, he loses a point, and players rotate one position to the left. When a player loses 5 points, he is out of the game. The last remaining player is the winner.

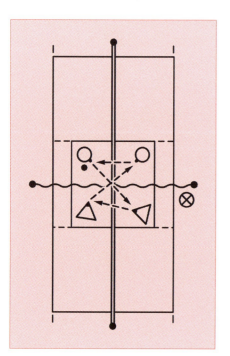

G62 Diagonal pass over Players are divided into pairs and stand on opposite sides of a net in 3-metre by 6-metre rectangular playing areas. One player from each pair stands in one half (3-metre by 3-metre square) of their playing area on each side of the net as shown. The ball must be passed diagonally to the opposing player on the other side of the net, who then passes the ball across to her partner (on the same side of the net), who then passes the ball diagonally back over the net to the opposing player, and so on. When one team commits an error, the opposing team gets a point. The first team to reach a certain number of points is the winner. *Variations*: (a) Another net or rope can be used to divide the rectangular playing areas between teammates on each side of the net; (b) players on the same side of the net switch positions after the ball crosses the net.

WITH AN OPPONENT

Attack defence

Coaching note

Attack defence is one of the most stimulating aspects of the game of volleyball. Spectacular efforts to prevent the ball from hitting the ground can motivate teammates and excite spectators. Technical skill as well as a determined attitude are requirements for defenders to be effective.

G63 **Boomerang** Three players position themselves in front of a large, smooth wall as shown. One player (defender) stands in a 3-metre by 3-metre playing area marked 2 metres away from the wall. Another player (attacker) stands on a box with a ball behind the square playing area. At the signal, the player standing on the box spikes the ball against the wall (the ball must bounce in the square playing area before hitting the wall). When the spiked ball rebounds off the wall, the defender must try to (forearm) pass the ball before it bounces, so it lands in the playing area. Each successful forearm pass earns a point for the defender. After each spike, the attacker becomes the defender, the defender rests, and a third player (who rested the previous round) replaces the attacker. After several rounds, the player with the most points is the winner.

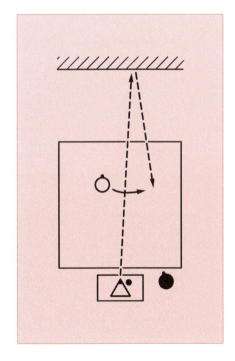

105

LEAD-UP GAMES

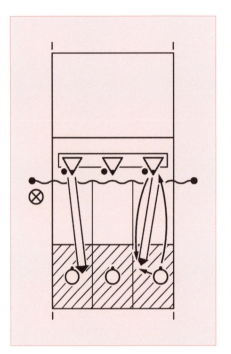

G64 Attack and defend one-on-one   Players are divided into two equal groups of attackers and defenders and position themselves on the court as shown. Three attacking players (each with a ball) stand on a bench 1 metre away from the net on one side of the net, while three defenders each occupy one of the three equal sections of the court on the other side of the net. At the signal, the attackers (one at a time) attack the ball over the net into the corresponding section of the court. An attacked ball cannot land between the net and the attack line. Defenders must try to prevent the ball from hitting the floor. If the ball touches the floor before the defender can get a hand on it, the attacker gets a point. If the defender is able to dig the ball, he gets a point and switches roles with the attacker. After a specified period of time, points are tallied to determine a winner.

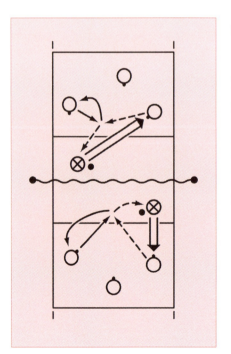

G65 Kojima   Three players position themselves on the volleyball court as shown. A coach stands on the same side of the net as the players, in either position 2 or 4. The coach attacks a ball at a player, who must pass the ball up in the air for another player to pass the ball to the coach. Players try to return to their initial starting positions as the coach then continues to attack the ball. Players stay in the drill either for a certain time period or until they are able to consecutively dig and pass the ball up to the coach a given number of times.

WITH AN OPPONENT

G66 **Five-player Kojima** Five players position themselves on the volleyball court as shown. Three players are in the backcourt and two players are at the net – one in position 2 and the other in position 4. One of the players at the net attacks a ball at one of the four players, who must pass the ball up in the air so another player can pass the ball to one of the outside corner positions at the net. Players try to return to their initial starting positions as the player at the net who receives the pass then continues to attack the ball. Players stay in the drill either for a certain time period or until they are able to consecutively dig and pass the ball successfully a given number of times.

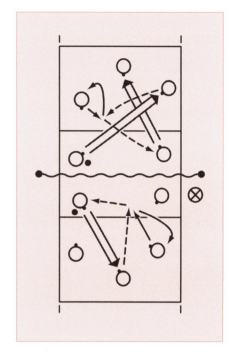

G67 **Cross-court attack** Four players position themselves on a volleyball court as shown, with another (lower) net or rope dividing the court lengthwise. Player 1 begins with the ball and sets the ball over the lengthwise rope to player 2; player 2 attacks the ball cross-court over the intersecting net and rope to player 3; player 3 tries to dig the ball; player 4 retrieves the ball and returns it to player 1. Players rotate one position to the left after every five attempts. The pattern continues until each player has played in every position at least once.

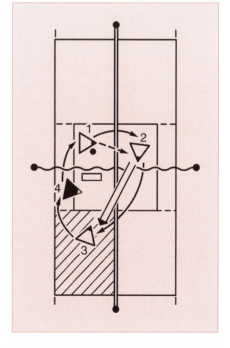

LEAD-UP GAMES

Developing advanced playing ability

Mini-games

> **Coaching note**
>
> *Mini-games of volleyball, with a smaller court size and/or fewer players, are excellent ways of developing playing ability. A smaller playing area makes a court easier to defend and requires greater ball control. Fewer players decreases confusion with regard to whose responsibility it is to make the play. Fewer players on the court also guarantees more contacts per player.*

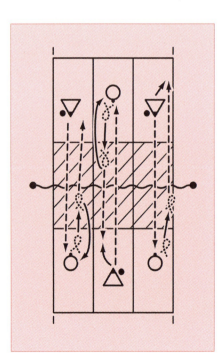

G68 One-on-one The volleyball court is divided into thirds lengthwise. The size of each side of the playing court is 9 metres long and 3 metres wide, with a ball landing inside the attack line (3 metres from each side of the centre line) deemed out of bounds. Two players begin on opposite sides of the net on each court. A rally begins with a two-hand underhand toss from behind the attack line over the net. A maximum of three contacts per side are allowed, and the winner of the rally scores a point and begins the next rally as indicated. The game is over when one player reaches a certain number of points. *Variations*: (a) Only volley pass and forearm pass contacts are allowed; (b) rallies begin with a serve; (c) the player leading after a certain time period is declared the winner.

ADVANCED PLAYING ABILITY

G69 Winners one-on-one   The set-up for this game is similar to G68, except that three or more players are to play on a lengthwise court. One side of the court is designated as the winner's side (W) and the other side is designated as the challenger's side (C). A challenger begins the rally with a serve. The winner of the rally goes to (or stays on) the winner's side. The loser of the rally goes to the end of the challenger's end line, while a new challenger begins the rally with a serve. A point is scored only when the player on the winner's side wins the rally. No point is awarded on a service error. The server goes to the end of the challenger's end line and a new challenger serves. The game is over when one player reaches a certain number of points. *Variation*: The player leading after a certain time period is declared the winner.

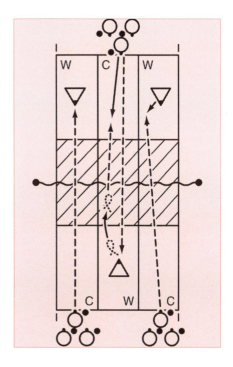

G70 Tournament one-on-one   The set-up and rules for this game are the same as G68. After a certain time period, the player with the most points is declared the winner. The winners of each court move one court to the right and the losers of each court move one court to the left. The winner on the far right court stays on that court and the loser on the far left court stays on that court. The next round of the tournament begins with a new opponent. The tournament continues for a given number of rounds. The tournament winner is the player who wins the game on the far right court (winner's court) after the last round. *Variation*: The set-up and rules are the same as G69. After a certain time period, the player(s) with the most points moves to a designated "winner's" court. The player(s) with the least points moves to another designated court, and the remainder are assigned to the last court. The players have now been tiered to play in the next tournament.

LEAD-UP GAMES

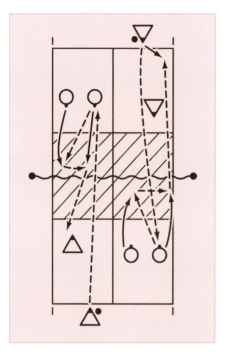

G71 Two-on-two   The volleyball court is divided in half lengthwise. The size of each side of the playing court is 9 metres long and 4.5 metres wide, with a ball landing inside the attack line (3 metres from each side of the centre line) deemed out of bounds. Two players begin on each side of the net on each court as shown. A rally begins with one player on each court serving from behind the end line. The receiving team must have both players in position ready to receive the serve. A maximum of three contacts per side are allowed. The team winning the rally scores a point and then serves to begin the next rally. The game is over when a team reaches a certain number of points. *Variations*: (a) Only volley pass and forearm pass contacts are allowed, with no blocking; (b) a ball landing inside the attack line is in bounds; (c) the team leading after a certain time period is declared the winner; (d) winners two-on-two (see G69); (e) tournament two-on-two (see G70).

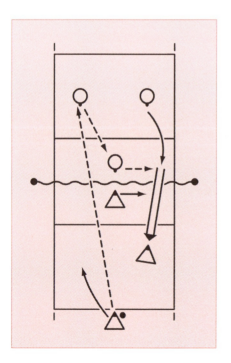

G72 Three-on-three   Players are positioned on the court as shown. The player at the net is designated as the middle blocker/setter. The other two players are designated as passers/diggers/attackers. The rally begins with one player serving from the end line. A maximum of three contacts per side are allowed. The winner scores a point and then serves to begin the next rally. If the receiving team wins the rally, players rotate positions clockwise. The game is over when a team reaches a certain number of points. *Variations*: (a) The team leading after a certain time period is declared the winner; (b) winners three-on-three (see G69).

ADVANCED PLAYING ABILITY

G73 Four-on-four Players are positioned on the court as shown. The rally begins with one player serving from the end line. A maximum of three contacts per side are allowed. The winner of the rally scores a point and then serves to begin the next rally. If the receiving team wins the rally, players rotate positions clockwise. The game is over when a team reaches a certain number of points. *Variation*: The team leading after a certain time period is declared the winner.

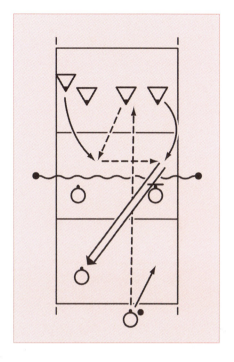

G74 Downball to attack four-on-four
Players begin in their initial defensive positions on the court as shown. One coach initiates a rally by hitting/tossing a downball over the net. Each team makes their appropriate movements (see Part III, "How to Play the Game," pages 48–53) until the rally ends. The winner of the rally scores a point. The next rally begins by the other coach hitting/tossing a downball over the net to the other side. Coaches continue alternating the initiation of the rally until one team reaches a certain number of points. *Variations*: (a) Downballs to initiate the rally are hit/tossed to the side that loses the rally; (b) downballs to initiate the rally are hit/tossed to the side that wins the rally.

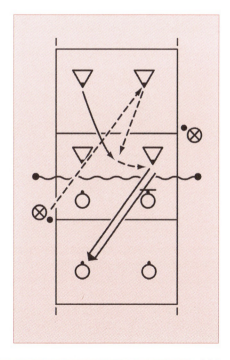

LEAD-UP GAMES

Games with opponents of unequal numbers

> **Coaching note**
>
> *Demands on players' abilities are increased with games involving teams of unequal numbers. Competitions with unequal numbers place players in situations where they must develop tactical and psychological abilities in order to be effective against a superior opponent.*

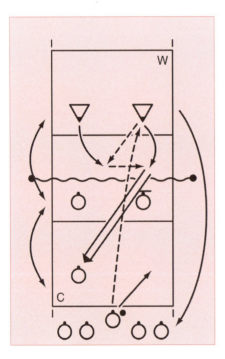

G75 Winners two-on-four Players begin on the court as shown. Two players are on the winner's side (W) while the challenger's side (C) has four players – two players at the net and two players in the backcourt. One backcourt player from the challenger's side begins the rally by serving. A maximum of three contacts per side are allowed. A point is scored only if the players on the winner's side win the rally. No point is scored on a missed serve. If the players on the winner's side win the rally, the two players in the frontcourt on the challenger's side rotate to go behind the end line of the challenger's court. The two players in the backcourt rotate to the frontcourt, and another two players from behind the end line rotate to go to the backcourt of the challenger's side. One of these players will begin the next rally by serving. If a serve is missed, no rotations occur, but the next player in line behind the challenger's end line replaces the player who made the service error.

This new player serves to begin the next rally. If the challengers win the rally, the players on the winner's side rotate to behind the end line of the challenger's side. On the challenger's side, the frontcourt rotates to the winner's side, and the backcourt rotates to the frontcourt. Another two players from behind the challenger's end line rotate to the backcourt of the challenger's side. One of these players will begin the next rally by serving. The game is over when a team reaches a certain number of points. *Variation*: The team leading after a certain time period is declared the winner.

ADVANCED PLAYING ABILITY

In any kind of competition there is always "the game within the game." Can the setter control the blockers? Can the attacker score against the defence? What other examples of "the game within the game" are there?

PART V

POSTURE AND MOVEMENT *119*

THE VOLLEY PASS *131*

THE FOREARM PASS *145*

DIGGING – BACKCOURT DEFENCE *151*

THE SERVE *155*

THE ATTACK *163*

THE BLOCK *169*

TEAM PLAY *173*

DRILLS

"How you practice is how you play!" and "Practice does not make perfect, practice makes permanent!" are well-known sayings in coaching. Skill is a prime requisite for volleyball performance. The most effective way to develop skill is the implementation of various drills in a practice environment. Effective practices with well-run drills at gamelike intensity levels are the essence of training and a key ingredient in today's coaching.

This section of the book is divided into subsections that present specific drills with the aim of developing a player's technical and tactical competitive skills and abilities. The following guidelines should be considered when implementing drills into the training program:

- Drills should have a specific purpose and be applicable to the skills used in the game.

- Drills should challenge the skill level of the players.

- Drills should be varied. The coach should choose from a number of different drills that accomplish the same purpose. Most practices should also include "fun" drills.

- Generally, drills should be carried out at a tempo that simulates the action of the game. Practices conducted at high intensity are more enjoyable for the athletes and provide a valuable carry-over into game situations.

- Drills that introduce complex skills must be practiced initially at a slower tempo. When the skill is perfected the tempo is correspondingly increased until it reaches or surpasses game intensity levels.

- Drills must be executed correctly. If the execution is not correct or a lack of effort is apparent, the coach must stop the activity and emphasize the correct method or demand the required training effort.

- Drills should flow from one to another with a minimum of time lost between them.

- Competition in drills increases athletes' interest and elevates the intensity of the practice.

- Each drill should be evaluated after practice to determine its overall effectiveness in attaining the desired goals.

DRILLS

Many components are involved in making drills exciting and motivating for athletes. Following are suggestions for consideration to add variety as well as establish success criteria (goals) in the various drills. Scoring suggestions for competitive drills may also be considered to keep athletes' focus and motivation at a high level.

Success criteria and scoring suggestions

- Execute skills for a given length of time.

- Execute skills for a given number of repetitions.

- Execute skills for a given number of successful repetitions.

- Execute skills for a given number of continuous successful repetitions.

- Increase physical and psychological demands by including tasks between skill repetitions (e.g., running, jumping, agility exercises, mental exercises).

- Place athletes in groups. The first group to successfully complete the drill is considered the winner.

- Use a plus and minus scoring system. A point is awarded for every successful execution, while a point is deducted for every error. The goal is to attain a designated overall score.

Practice management considerations

Efficiency – Take into account the number of athletes involved in the drills, the number of repetitions or contacts made, and the number of successful repetitions or contacts (quality of performance).

Feedback – Simple word cues or phrases should be established to minimize time to trigger corrective responses in players.

Overload – Athletes should do a large number of repetitions. Therefore, there should be at least one ball per player.

Reversibility – "If you don't use it, you lose it." Skill proficiency is decreased if the skill is ignored in practice.

OVERVIEW

Specificity – To effectively transfer skills to the game, drills should mirror particular game situations as closely as possible.

Structure – Drills should be designed to ensure optimal use of court space and personnel. Shaggers are assigned when appropriate.

Success – Success is a key motivator. Drill difficulty should be manipulated to achieve an appropriate level of success.

Training variables – Drills should be manipulated according to the training variables of intensity, duration, and frequency.

Variety – Subtle changes in drills can improve intensity. Manipulate goals, tasks, and scoring criteria.

> In all things, success depends on previous preparation, and without such preparation there is sure to be failure.
>
> *Confucius*

DRILLS

Chart 1

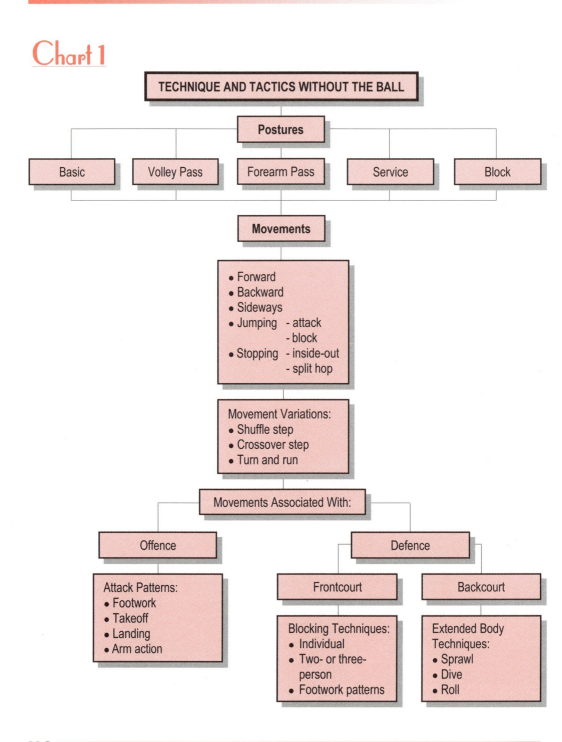

Posture and movement

Posture and movement can be viewed as important building blocks to successful skill execution. While posture is considered a foundation to the proper execution of skills, movement places a player in the correct court position to execute the skills.

> ### The different volleyball postures include
> 1. basic volleyball posture
> 2. forearm pass posture
> 3. volley pass posture
> 4. service posture ("statue")
> 5. block posture ("caribou")

Basic volleyball posture

The following are components of the *basic volleyball posture*:

- Feet shoulder-width apart with one foot slightly ahead of the other
- Toes pointed straight ahead or slightly inward, which helps keep the weight forward
- Back straight but bent at the waist with a forward tilt
- Shoulders and arms relaxed, elbows straight
- Hands resting on knees/thighs or loosely clutching shorts

Players utilize this posture between rallies to either rest or to wait for the whistle to be blown to begin the next rally.

DRILLS

Volley pass posture

The *volley pass posture* is the preparatory posture to execute a volley pass. This posture has the body in an erect position. Feet are less than shoulder-width apart and almost parallel to each other. The back is relatively straight with a slight tilt forward. Hands are held in a cupped position slightly above the hairline of the forehead.

Forearm pass posture

The *forearm pass posture* is used just before the execution of a forearm pass. Forearm pass posture is a slight variation of the basic volleyball posture. From the basic volleyball posture, the knees are brought forward. The hands are lifted from the knees/thighs, and the angle of the back is elevated. The arms are relatively straight, with hands above the knees/thighs and palms facing each other.

In other situations, athletes can get into the forearm pass posture by using a preparatory "split hop" to posture. The split hop prepares the body for sudden short movements to get to the ball.

Service posture

The *service posture*, or "statue," is the posture the player assumes in preparation for executing the serve. There are slight variations of the service posture depending on whether the athlete is executing an underhand, sidearm, overhand, or jump serve.

In the underhand service posture, the player stands with feet together with the body facing the target. The ball is held slightly ahead of the body at hip level in the nonhitting hand.

In the sidearm service posture, the player stands perpendicular to the target. Feet are together, and the volleyball is held in the nonhitting hand, with the arm straight ahead of the body and parallel to the floor. The hitting arm is parallel to the ground, making a 90-degree angle with the nonhitting arm.

In the overhand service posture, the player stands perpendicular to the target. The arms make a "U" shape, with hands held high and elbows at eye level. The line joining the hands and head is directed toward the intended target.

In the jump service posture, the player faces the target. One foot is ahead of the other, and the body lean is forward. The volleyball can be held a variety of ways, either with both hands or in either hand.

POSTURE AND MOVEMENT

Block posture

In the **block posture**, or "caribou," the player stands at the net. Feet are parallel to the net and slightly wider than shoulder-width apart. The knees are comfortably flexed, the back is straight, and hands are held above and slightly in front of the head. Arms are spread with fingers apart and stiff, palms facing the net.

Progressions for posture

1. Players form pairs. The coach directs the players to get into the basic volleyball posture. The players face each other, observing and correcting the posture as the coach calls out the components.

2. In pairs, players face each other as they assume the correct forearm pass posture. They then engage in a "knee slap" game, with the objective being to touch the other player on the inside of the knee. Posture must be maintained as coaches watch out for "flying fannies" and "lunge" movements.

3. Players face the coach. When the coach claps hands, the players "split hop" to posture. This is then combined with the various movements. Coaches ensure that the players have their weight forward when in posture by asking the players to lift one foot. The players should then fall forward.

Movement

Movement is often required before executing the skills of the game. Movement is directed either forward, backward, or some variation to either side. All movement should begin and end with the body in an appropriate posture, thus providing a foundation to execute the skills.

Components and types of movement include

- adjustment of height and location of the centre of gravity with respect to the base of support
- weight transfer to initiate movement
- shuffle step
- crossover step
- turn and run
- stop; inside-out footwork (inside step to break and outside step to balance)

DRILLS

Progressions for movement

1. Players face the coach. The coach directs the players to slowly run forward. On the whistle the players stop by "split hopping" to forearm pass or volley pass posture. The same is done with backward movement.

2. Players face the coach. The coach points in the direction the players should utilize the shuffle technique. On the whistle the players stop, using inside-out footwork to get into one of the passing postures.

3. Same as 2 but the players work on a simple crossover step, crossing one foot in front of the other and ending up with inside-out footwork to get into a passing posture.

4. Same as 2 but the players initiate movement with a weight transfer or a short step in the direction they want to go, then turn and run. On the whistle the players use inside-out footwork to get into basic posture and once again face the coach.

5. Same as 2 but the coach can point in any direction, and the players can use any movement variation they wish.

6. Specific movement drills parallel to the net will be covered in the section on jumping.

Posture and movement drills

D1 Cut the ball off – Roll   Players form pairs, with one ball. One player rolls the ball slowly to either side of his partner. The partner focuses on a movement variation to place himself in a position so that the ball can roll between his feet. The partner then rolls the ball back to either side of the first player so that he can work on his movement skills.

D2 Cut the ball off – Toss   Same as D1 but the ball is tossed underhand and the partner must move to catch the ball underhand, focusing on the movement skills.

D3 Bounce between the legs   The coach is on one side of the net, and half the athletes are in single file on the other side of the court. The remaining players shag and hand balls. The coach easily tosses the ball (with a low trajectory) over the net. The first player in line must quickly move to the ball so that it bounces between her legs. This is repeated for each player in the line for a given number of times.

POSTURE AND MOVEMENT

Running drills

The lines of the volleyball court are used as start lines or markers for the various movements or races. The individual or team winner is determined by who completes the given task first.

A whistle can be used as an auditory start signal. However other start signals, such as dropping a ball, can be used. For variety, players can start lying on their stomachs, on their backs, or in any other appropriate position. All movements are done as quickly as possible. When a line is part of the drill, a foot or a hand must touch the line.

D4 **Back and forth**   Start at the end line. Players run forward to the centre line, backward to the attack line, forward to the second attack line (on the other side of the court), backward to the centre line, and forward to the opposite end line.

D5 **Back and forth – Sprawl**   Players start at the end line lying on their stomachs. They run to the centre line, executing a front sprawl or dive before touching the line. They return to the initial end line, executing a front sprawl or dive before touching the line. Finally, players run to the opposite end line, executing a sprawl or dive when crossing the line.

D6 **Net and back**   Start at the attack line. Players run forward to the centre line, then backward to the original attack line. This is repeated a given number of times (6 to 10 times is suggested).

D7 **Back to attack**   Begin at the attack line. Players run to the centre line, do a half turn, and run backward to the other attack line. Continue 6 to 10 times.

D8 **Circle sprint**   Players in pairs are positioned at different locations on the court (four pairs at the points where the sidelines and attack lines meet; two pairs on each end line at the midpoint between the sidelines). On the signal one player in each pair crawls through his partner's legs then runs around the court in a clockwise fashion (everyone runs in the same direction). Each player returns to his partner, crawls between his legs, then retrieves a ball from the middle of the court. There should be one ball fewer than the number of pairs in the circle. The team without a ball must do a contingency (e.g., five push-ups).

D9 **Face the net**   Players run from corner to corner of one side of the court, always facing the net. Sideways movement is done with a shuffle step.

DRILLS

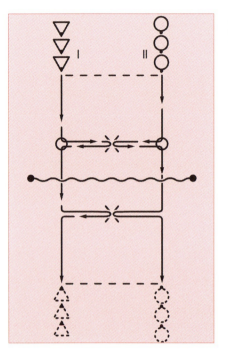

D10 **Next in line** Two teams stand as shown. One member of each team runs according to the lines in the diagram. The X in the middle of the attack line has to be touched by one foot. The next player in line can start when the first one crosses under the net. Players must face the net at all times.

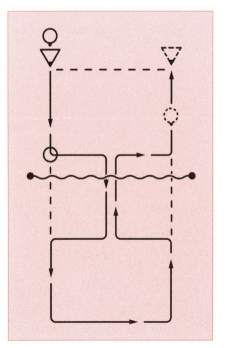

D11 **Chase** Two runners have the same distance to run. The second runner starts when the first one reaches the circled area. Players must face the net at all times. The goal is for the second runner to get closer than 6 metres to the first one. Afterwards, the roles are changed.

POSTURE AND MOVEMENT

Jumping drills

Attacking and blocking are technical volleyball skills that are executed in relation to a ball; however they can be practiced without a ball. The following attacking and blocking exercises enhance body coordination, endurance, and jumping ability.

A block jump is counted when the heel of the hand goes higher than the upper edge of the net. To encourage even greater jumping effort, an elastic or rope can be strung at an appropriate height above the net. The heel of the hand must go higher than the elastic or rope.

D12 Simple block   Begin at the net in block posture. Players block jump on the spot, go underneath the net, then block jump on the other side of the net. Repeat 6 to 10 times.

Variations:

(a) Two players begin in block posture, facing each other. Without touching the net, the players block jump and clap each other's hands together as hard as they can above the net. Repeat 6 to 10 times, with players either remaining on the side they began on or going underneath the net to change sides for the next jump.

(b) Players begin by sitting on a bench that is parallel to and 2 metres away from the net. On a signal from the coach, they execute a block jump from this beginning position.

(c) Players begin by standing with their shoulders perpendicular to the net or with their backs facing the net. On a signal, players execute a block jump, land facing the net, then return to their original positions.

D13 Attack line to block   Begin at the attack line. On a signal, players run underneath the net, do a half turn to get into block posture facing the net, then execute a block jump. On landing, they then run backward to the other attack line. Repeat 6 to 10 times.

DRILLS

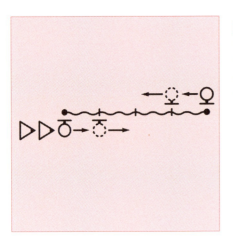

D14 Shuffle step to block   Players begin at the net near the sideline of the court. Moving sideways using the shuffle step, five block jumps are executed. The jump areas can be marked with antennae or coloured ribbons.

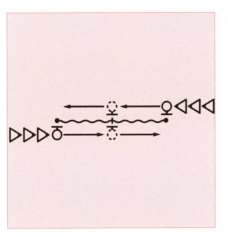

D15 Crossover step to block   Same as D14 but players use the crossover step and execute three block jumps, one near the sideline where the player begins, one at the middle of the net, and the third near the other sideline. The player then runs back to the original sideline. This can be done as a relay in groups.

D16 Simple attack approach   Players begin at the attack line in position 4. They approach the net using proper spike jump footwork. Continue from position 3 and then from position 2. Repeat.

D17 Attack approach – Block response   One set of players begins at the attack line in positions 4, 3, and 2. Another set of players begins on the opposite side of the net in block posture in positions 4, 3, and 2. Block jumps are done as a reaction to the attack movement. The roles of the attacker and blocker are then reversed.

POSTURE AND MOVEMENT

Movement drills for backcourt defence

D18 Sitting ball test   Medicine balls are placed on the corners and middle of each rectangular area as marked. The player begins by sitting on a medicine ball in the middle of the rectangle. On the signal the player runs to corner 1, does a 180-degree turn, quickly sits on the medicine ball in corner 1, runs to the middle, turns to face corner 2, sits on the medicine ball, runs to corner 2, does a 180-degree turn, quickly sits on the medicine ball in corner 2, returns to the middle, and so on. This continues until the player returns to the middle after all four corners have been touched. Players can be timed, or races can be conducted with players beginning on different rectangular courts.

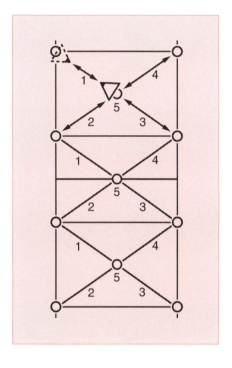

D19 Line touches   Players stand between the attack line and the centre line. On the signal, the players alternately touch each line with their outside hands. Count the number of line touches in a given time period (15 or 30 seconds is recommended).

D20 Sideline shuttle   While facing the net, players run from sideline to sideline, touching the line with a hand. As an alternative, players can start by lying on their sides, their stomachs, or their backs.

D21 Extended body movements   Practice extended body movements from a low and wide forearm pass posture with balls. As players extend and contact the ground, they grab the ball and scoop it up. Players return to the original posture as fast as possible and begin again. Work the other side.

DRILLS

Combined movement drills

D22 Complex exercises without a ball Half the players begin lying on their stomachs with noses on one end line; the other half begin similarly on the other end line. One group does what the coach requests while the other group rests. The players perform a specific movement task or group of movement tasks, jog to the net, then run slowly backward to their original end line.

Movement tasks:

- feet pitter-patter (five low, five high)
- sprawl forward
- knee tuck
- back roll
- Russian kick
- front roll
- spike jump
- block jump

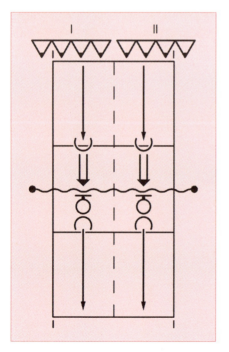

D23 Position change with movement tasks
Each group of players can move on only half of a lengthwise court. The coach outlines what task must be performed at the end line, at the attack line, and at the net. As an example, players begin on the end line lying on their stomachs. On the signal they run to the attack line and execute a sprawl, get up and do a spike jump approach, do a block jump at the net, do a back roll, turn to face the original end line, sprint to this end line, and do a dive. The coach indicates with a whistle when the next group of players is to begin. The groups end up at their original end line.

POSTURE AND MOVEMENT

D24 **Mirror image**   Players line up on each end line. Player A moves into the court and performs several volleyball-specific movements (block jumps, spike jumps, extended body dig movements, sprints, turns, and so on). Player B must immediately mirror these movements. This occurs for up to 15 seconds, and then the coach whistles for two other players to move into the court. The coach designates the new mover and imitator.

Posture is the foundation of the proper execution of skills.

DRILLS

Chart 2

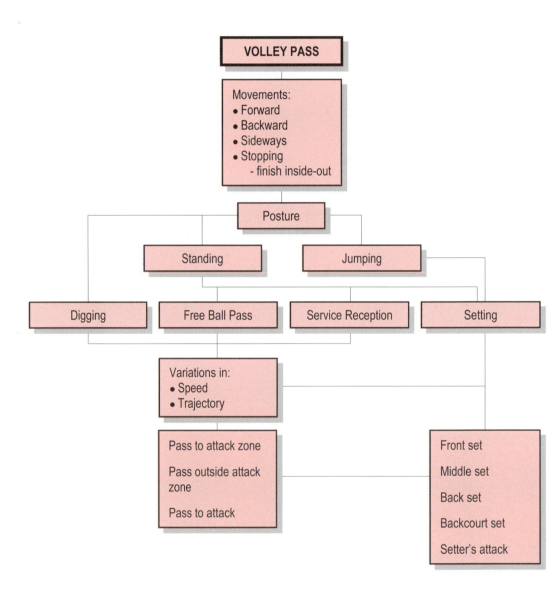

130

# The volley pass

The volley pass is the passing skill in which the ball is contacted with both hands above the head. It is the skill most often used to deliver the ball to an attacker. It is also used in situations (free balls) where the trajectory of the incoming ball allows for contact above the head. More recently, ball handling rules have been liberalized to allow for the use of the volley pass when contacting the ball either from a serve or an attack. Although all players must be adept at this skill, it is the setter who must have superior mastery.

The following are components of the *volley pass*:

- **Posture** – The body is erect, knees slightly bent, feet close together, either parallel or one foot slightly ahead of the other. Hands are above the hairline of the forehead, with elbows comfortably flexed.

- **Hand position (shape)** – Fingers are spread, allowing the hands to form a bowl shape in order to fit around the ball. Thumbs and index fingers are almost touching, with the wrists cocked back (90 degrees). Thumbs are pointed to the opposite shoulders.

- **Body position** – The body should be in a stable and balanced position (posture), facing the target so that the ball is contacted above the head. Facing the target indicates that feet, knees, hips, and shoulders are aligned with a target that is directly ahead of the body.

- **Contact point** – The ball is contacted by the hands, primarily with the pads of the fingers and edges of the thumbs. The ball does **NOT** make contact with the palms or the ends of the fingers.

- **Passing action** – On ball contact, the ball causes the fingers and thumbs to bend backward and absorb any downward momentum. The elbows and knees extend upward and in the direction of the intended pass. The follow-through is such that the elbows and knees are fully extended, and the shape of the wrists and hands is maintained.

Word cues and phrases for the volley pass include

1. beat the ball
2. face the target
3. shape early
4. extend

DRILLS

The elbows and knees extend upward and in the direction of the intended pass. The follow-through is such that the elbows and knees are fully extended, and the shape of the wrists and hands is maintained.

VOLLEY PASS

Technique and control drills — Individual

For these drills, the players pass the ball repeatedly to themselves. Players should have their own balls. These drills should be changed frequently to maximize concentration and quality of execution.

D25 **Self volley**   Players volley the ball to themselves on the same spot, keeping the height the ball is passed consistent.

Variation: Players alternate low and high passes.

D26 **One-hand volley**   Players volley the ball to themselves using only one hand then the other hand.

Variation: Players alternate hands.

D27 **Volley with task**   After every pass, players do a small task such as glancing at an object, clapping hands, touching a body part, turning 90 degrees, doing a half squat.

D28 **Volley lying down**   Players lie on their backs while passing to themselves.

D29 **Volley with posture change**   Players change their posture while passing (e.g., go from standing to lying on their backs to standing again).

D30 **Volley with court line movement**   Players volley the ball to themselves while walking along the court lines.

D31 **Volley with movement and turn**   Players volley the ball forward 3 metres, volley to themselves, do a half turn, volley forward 3 metres so that they return to the original position, and volley to themselves. Repeat.

D32 **Beat the ball**   Players volley the ball forward 4 to 6 metres with a high arc, letting the ball bounce only once. In the meantime, they get into position as quickly as possible to volley the ball back to the original starting position. Repeat.

D33 **Distance volleys**   Players take six volleys to go from sideline to sideline. Repeat, decreasing the number of volleys to go from sideline to sideline by one each time.

DRILLS

D34 **Volley shot**   Players volley the ball to themselves and then volley into a basketball hoop. Increase the distance away from the hoop.

D35 **Volley against the wall**   Players stand 1 to 4 metres away from a wall and volley the ball against the wall.

Variation: Players volley to themselves before volleying against the wall.

Using the net as an obstacle

D36 **Line to line over the net**   Players volley the ball to themselves while moving from attack line to opposite attack line. They play the ball over the net while crawling underneath.

D37 **Over and under**   Beginning at one sideline, players stand perpendicular to the net and repeatedly pass the ball over the net while crawling underneath. They continue along the full length of the net.

D38 **Waves**   Players line up in groups of three along one end line. They walk to the other end, volleying the ball as they go. At the net players go underneath, while passing the ball underneath the net as well. They continue to the opposite end line. Here, they catch their balls and quickly run outside the court to line up again at the original end line. The next group in line starts when the group ahead reaches the net.

Variations:

(a)   Pass the ball over the net while going underneath.

(b)   Players count the number of volleys to go from end line to end line. Decrease the number of contacts with each repetition wave.

(c)   Players race to the opposite end line and back. Fastest while controlling the ball wins.

Technique and control drills – Partners

D39 **Partner volley sitting**   Players form pairs and sit on the ground 1 metre apart, facing each other. They volley the ball back and forth.

Variations:

(a) Players volley first to themselves and then to their partners.

(b) Players perform a task after volleying to their partners. The task can be a sit-up, back roll (only lifting feet above head), and so on.

D40 **Partner volley on stomachs**   Players lie on their stomachs 1 metre apart and volley the ball to each other, lifting their upper bodies by arching their backs.

D41 **Simple partner volley**   One player stands at the net, the other at the attack line. They volley the ball back and forth.

Variations:

(a) Players stand on either side of the net, about 1 metre away from the net. They volley the ball to each other.

(b) Players volley first to themselves and then to their partners.

(c) Players volley to themselves and then perform a task after volleying to their partners. Task suggestions include

- with two hands, touching the ankles, then knees, then hips, then shoulders
- doing a 90-degree jump turn and then jumping back (increase to 180 degrees and 360 degrees)
- sitting down
- doing a push-up
- sprawling to the side
- doing a back roll
- identifying the number of fingers a partner holds up (after volleying to self)

D42 **Partner volley with posture change**   During the volleys, the players change from standing to kneeling, to sitting, to lying, and back up again.

DRILLS

D43 Pass to me   After each pass, a player moves to another spot on the court.

D44 Volley pass with hurdle jump   Players stand 6 metres apart and volley the ball to each other five times. They give the ball to a second pair and proceed to jump over two hurdles. They then run back and take the ball, and the second pair goes over the hurdles.

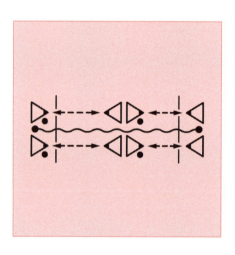

D45 Parallel net volleying   Players volley parallel to the net.

D46 Two ball   Players stand 6 metres apart. There are two balls in the drill. One ball is volleyed while the other ball is rolled back and forth.

Variation: Players bounce the second ball or toss and catch it.

VOLLEY PASS

Movement drills – Partners

D47 **Follow your partner**   Players begin 1 metre apart midway between the net and the end line. One player (A) begins by volleying the ball to her partner (B). Player A then runs to the end line and back. Player B volleys on the spot to herself and then back to player A at the same location. Player A volleys back to player B and then runs to the net and back. Player B volleys to herself and then back to player A. Repeat.

Variation: Both players are moving. When player A receives the ball from player B, he volleys on the spot to himself before volleying back to player B. Player B then will also move to the end line (or net) and back.

D48 **To and fro**   Players stand on either side of the net, at the attack line. They volley to themselves as they move toward the net, then they volley to their partners. They lightly touch the net and run backward to the attack line.

D49 **Back and forth shuffle**   Players stand near one sideline on either side of the net, about 1 metre away from the net. They volley the ball over the net to each other as they shuffle sideways to the other sideline.

D50 **Move to pass it back**   Players in net positions 2, 3, and 4 stand with their backs to the net. Their partners start near the end line. The net players volley the ball in such a way that the players at the end line must run forward or to the side to get to the ball. The ball must be volleyed back to the original net position.

Jump setting is an advanced technical and tactical skill.

DRILLS

Group drills

D51 Diagonal passing Players face each other standing diagonally to the net in positions 2 and 5 or 4 and 1. The player at the net (2 or 4) makes her partner move slightly by varying the location of the volley. The ball is volleyed back.

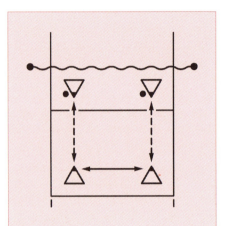

D52 Criss-cross Players stand facing each other in positions 2 and 1, as well as positions 4 and 5. The players in positions 2 and 4 remain where they are, whereas players in positions 1 and 5 change places after each volley. Begin by having the players at the net volley to themselves and then to their partners. The players in positions 1 and 5 return the volleys and proceed to change places.

Variation: Net players can also change places.

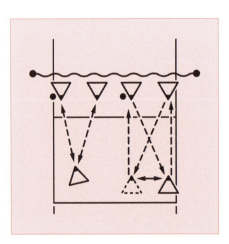

D53 Face the target Three players form a triangle (positions 2, 3, and 1 or 4, 3, and 5). The player in position 4 (2) volleys the ball to the player in position 5 (1), who volleys it to the player in position 3. The player in position 3 returns the ball to the player in position 5 (1), who then volleys it back to the player in position 4 (2).

Variations:

(a) Players in positions 4 (2) and 3 each have a ball and alternately pass it to the player in position 5 (1). The player in position 5 (1) returns the pass (this increases the speed of the drill).

(b) The backcourt player moves along the end line and must return diagonal passes to the other players at the net.

VOLLEY PASS

D54 **Triangles**   Triangles are formed with players in positions 4, 3, and 5 or 2, 6, and 1. The ball is passed in a triangle, ensuring that the passer is facing the target.

Variation: The triangle position where the first pass originates will have two players. After passing the ball, the player will follow the passed ball. To practice longer distance passes, positions 4, 2, and 5 (1) are used.

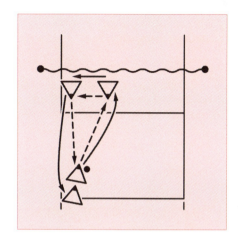

D55 **Pass parallel to the net**   Two players begin at the sideline in position 1. A third player, with a ball, starts at the net in position 3. The player in position 3 volleys the ball parallel to the net to position 2. One of the players in position 1 runs to the net, turns to become perpendicular to the net (to face the target), and passes the ball back to the player in position 3.

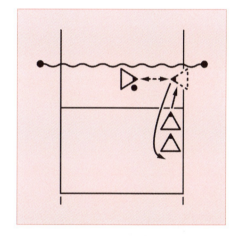

D56 **Volley two-on-two**   Two groups of two players stand behind the attack line about 3 metres apart on either side of the net. The ball is passed to the net, and the partner runs and volleys it over the net. The players on the other side decide who will pass the first ball to the net and the action is repeated. The order of who passes can be either random or predetermined (a).

Variation: The movement distances can be increased as well as every pass going across the net must be a jump volley (b).

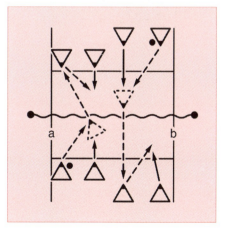

DRILLS

Back volley drills

D57 Middle passes back   Three players begin in positions 4, 3, and 2, about 1 metre away from the net (the attack line, end line, or any other line can be used for orientation purposes). Players in positions 2 and 4 pass the ball to the player in position 3. The player in position 3 will always face where the ball is being passed from and will use the back volley to pass it to the third player.

Variations:

(a) The player in position 3 does not turn around but always faces position 2 or 4. In this situation, the player who receives the back volley must pass the ball over the player in 3, to the other sideline.

(b) Before passing the ball, the player has to do a block jump at the net.

D58 End of the line   Four players stand in a line 1 to 2 metres apart. The first player back volleys to the second player and then runs to get behind the fourth player. The second player now becomes the first, and the drill continues.

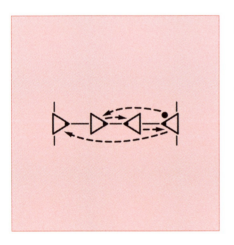

D59 Random back volley   Four players stand in such a manner that the two inner and the two outer players are facing each other. The players pass the ball randomly among each other, thus the back volley is used when necessary.

D60 Turn and back volley   Two players face each other. One player begins by volleying to himself, does a half turn, and then back volleys to his partner. The second player repeats this action.

VOLLEY PASS

D61 Parallel passing net and back Three players stand on the attack line 3 metres apart. The ball must be passed parallel to the net to another player. After passing the ball, the player must touch the net and return to her original position.

Variation: Two players start from the position where the first pass originates. After passing the ball, the player must touch the net and go to the position that he passed the ball to.

D62 Pass and position switch Three players begin as shown. Player B begins on the sideline and passes to a target, which will force player A to move forward about 4 metres. Player B moves behind player C. Player A back volleys the ball to player C and then runs to player B's original position to receive a return pass from player C. Player B moves to take player C's place and player A (who has replaced player B) passes to player C (who has replaced player A).

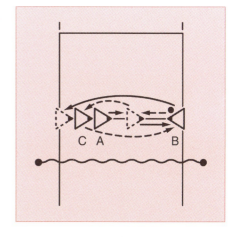

D63 Volley and go Two groups stand facing each other on opposite sides of a net. The first player on each side stands in a small square playing area as shown. The ball is passed over the net by the first player on one side to the first player on the other side. The ball must clear the net with one contact and must be played within the square boundaries. Once the ball is passed over the net, that player must run under the net to join the end of the line on the other side. This pattern continues until someone commits an error. When a player commits two errors, he is out of the drill. The last remaining player wins.

Variations:

(a) Players pass to themselves once before sending the ball back over the net.

(b) After passing the ball once to themselves, players complete a half turn and back volley the ball over the net.

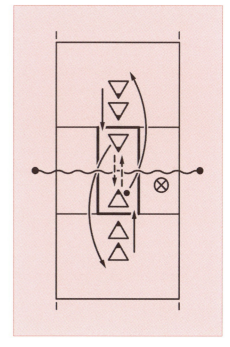

141

DRILLS

D64 Pass to position 3   Players begin in positions 4, 3, and 1. The player in position 1 passes the ball to the player in position 3. The player in position 3 back volleys to the player in position 4. The player in position 4 passes the ball to the player in position 1, and so on.

Variations:

(a) Two players start in position 1. Players follow the ball after executing a pass.

(b) The player in position 3 begins at the attack line and runs to the net in preparation to execute the back volley.

Application of the volley pass in mini-games

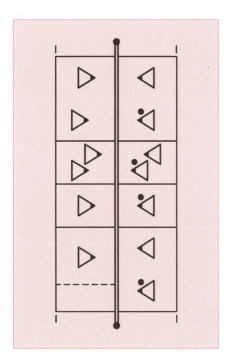

D65 Mini-game volleys   Mini-games can contribute to the development of game abilities very quickly. Beginning players can become familiar with various game situations and are then able to execute techniques and tactics in an appropriate manner. The volley pass can be trained in these mini-games (one-on-one, one-on-two, or two-on-two situations), utilizing different court dimensions.

For more information on mini-games see Part III, "How to Play the Game," beginning on page 43.

VOLLEY PASS

Shaping of the hands early in the execution of the volley pass enhances the probability of success.

DRILLS

Chart 3

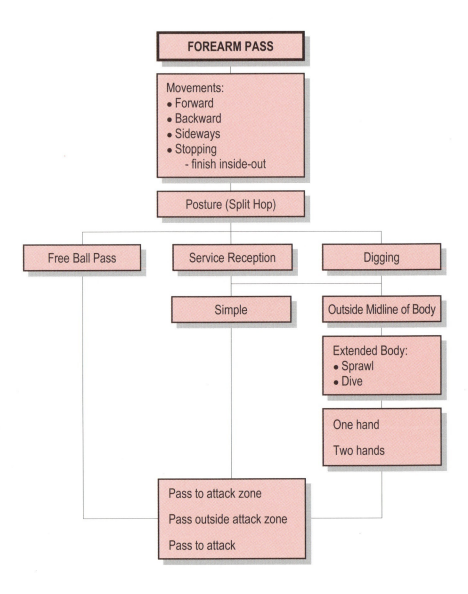

The forearm pass

The forearm pass is considered by volleyball experts to be the most important skill in the game of volleyball. The level of play of a match is most often determined by a team's ability to execute the forearm pass. It is the skill most often used on the first contact of the ball, whether it is service reception or passing an opponent's attack.

The following are components of the *forearm pass*:

- **Posture** – The feet are shoulder-width apart, with one foot slightly ahead of the other. Knees are comfortably flexed. The back is straight, with a slight tilt forward.

- **Arm position** – The arms are relatively straight, held to the sides above the thighs with palms facing each other.

- **Body position** – On contact of the ball by the opponent, most passers use a preparatory split hop to posture movement and then react to the oncoming ball. The feet are wide apart, and the body is aligned so that an appropriate rebound angle is established with the forearms. The hands are held with thumbs together and down.

- **Contact point** – The ball is contacted in the grooves of the forearms between the elbows and the wrists. Ideal contact is in the midline of the body, with the legs adjusting the height of the centre of gravity so that the ball is contacted at a level even with the belly button. When the ball is outside the midline, the shoulders dip to establish an appropriate rebound platform.

- **Passing action** – On contact the shoulders slightly rotate to push or "bunt" the ball to the target with an acceptable trajectory. The legs are used minimally.

Word cues and phrases for the forearm pass include

1. split hop to posture
2. arms straight then together
3. platform
4. rebound angle

DRILLS

Technique and control drills – Individual

Drills outlined in the section on the volley pass can be adapted and used to develop the forearm pass. Many of the drills in this section are similar to drills used for the volley pass.

D66 **Self pass**   Players pass the ball to themselves within the midline and outside the midline of the body.

Variations:

(a) Players alternate height of the pass.

(b) Players alternate between a volley pass and a forearm pass.

(c) Players alternate passing and letting the ball bounce off the floor.

D67 **Wall pass**   Players pass the ball against a wall.

Variation: Players use a forearm pass to receive the ball from the wall and use a volley pass to direct the ball to the wall.

D68 **One-arm passing**   Players pass the ball to themselves using one arm and then the other arm.

Variation: Players alternate arms.

D69 **Pass with task**   After every pass, players perform a small task such as glancing at an object, clapping hands, touching a body part, turning 90 degrees, doing a half squat.

D70 **Pass with court line movement**   Players pass the ball to themselves while walking along the court lines.

D71 **Pass and turn**   Players pass the ball forward 3 metres, pass to themselves, turn, pass the ball forward 3 metres so that the players return to the original position, then pass the ball to themselves. Repeat. *Note*: Players should pass from the midline as well as outside the midline of the body.

FOREARM PASS

D72 **Distance passes**   Players take six passes to go from sideline to sideline. Repeat, decreasing the number of forearm passes to go from sideline to sideline by one each time. Movement can be forward, facing the sideline, or using a shuffle step at 90 degrees to the sideline.

D73 **Pass to score**   Players begin by tossing the ball in the air, then forearm pass the ball into a basketball hoop.

Variations:

(a) Players begin by volleying the ball to themselves.

(b) Players begin by bouncing the ball off the floor.

(c) Players begin by tossing the ball against the backboard.

Using the net as an obstacle

D74 **Line to line over the net**   Players pass the ball to themselves while moving from attack line to opposite attack line. They play the ball over the net while crawling underneath.

D75 **Over and under**   Beginning at one sideline, players stand with their shoulders perpendicular to the net and repeatedly pass the ball over the net while crawling underneath. They continue along the full length of the net.

D76 **Waves**   Players line up in groups of three along one end line. They side shuffle to the other end, passing the ball as they go. They go underneath the net and pass the ball over the net. They continue to the opposite end line. Here, they catch their balls and quickly run outside the court to line up again at the original end line. The next group in line starts when the group ahead reaches the net.

DRILLS

Technique and control drills — Partners

D77 Simple partner passing   One player stands at the net, the other between the end line and the attack line. The player at the net easily tosses the ball, and her partner forearm passes the ball back to the net.

Variations:

(a) After passing the ball, the second player runs backward and touches the end line.

(b) After passing the ball, the second player runs to the net and touches the ball in the first player's hands.

(c) Players pass the ball back and forth.

(d) Players pass first to themselves and then to their partners.

Movement drills — Partners

D78 Follow your partner   Players begin 1 metre apart midway between the net and the end line. One player (A) begins by passing the ball to his partner (B). Player A then runs to the end line and back. Player B passes to himself and then back to player A. Player A passes back to player B and then runs to the net and back. Player B passes to himself and then back to player A. Repeat.

Variation: Both players are moving. When player A receives the ball from player B, she then passes to herself before passing back to player B. Player B then will also move to the end line (or net) and back.

D79 Partner waves   Players line up in pairs, facing each other, along one end line. They pass the ball back and forth as they side shuffle to the other end line. They go underneath the net and pass the ball over the net, then continue to the opposite end line. Players catch their balls and quickly run outside the court to line up again at the original end line. The next group in line starts when the group ahead reaches the net.

D80 Back and forth shuffle   Players stand near one sideline on either side of the net, about 1 metre away from the net. They pass the ball over the net to each other as they shuffle sideways to the other sideline.

FOREARM PASS

D81 To and fro Players stand on either side of the net, about 1 metre away from the net. They forearm pass the ball to each other. After they pass, they quickly move to lightly touch the net and then return to their original positions.

Variation: Players stand on either side of the net, at the attack line. They forearm pass to themselves as they move toward the net, then they volley to their partners. They lightly touch the net and run backward to the attack line.

Group drills

D82 Shuttle pass Groups of players stand in a line on either side of the net. The first player in one line passes the ball over the net and then proceeds to the end of the line on the other side of the net. The first player on the other side of the net passes the ball back over the net and then proceeds to the end of the line on the other side of the net. The next player in line continues the drill, and so on.

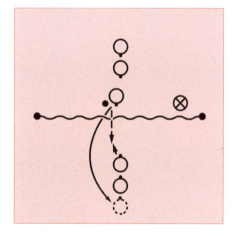

D83 Criss-cross Players stand facing each other in positions 2 and 1, as well as positions 4 and 5. The players in positions 2 and 4 remain where they are, whereas players in positions 1 and 5 change places after each volley. Begin by having the players at the net volley to themselves and then to their partners. The players in positions 1 and 5 return the volleys and proceed to change places.

Variation: Net players can also change places.

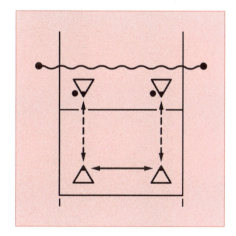

DRILLS

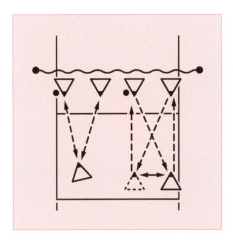

D84 **Face the target** Three players form a triangle (positions 2, 3, and 1 or 4, 3, and 5). The player in position 4 (2) passes the ball to the player in position 5 (1), who passes it to the player in position 3. The player in position 3 returns the ball to the player in position 5 (1), who then passes it back to the player in position 4 (2).

Variations:

(a) Players in positions 4 (2) and 3 each have a ball and alternately pass it to the player in position 5 (1). The player in position 5 (1) returns the pass (this increases the speed of the drill).

(b) Similar to above but the backcourt player moves along the end line and must return diagonal passes to the other players at the net.

Forearm pass posture is a foundation from which the player can either pass the serve or dig attacked balls.

Digging – Backcourt defence

Digging, or backcourt defence, fulfills a prime objective of the game of volleyball – to prevent the ball from contacting the floor. The specific functions include digging hard-hit spikes and recovering deflections, tips, and roll shots. Most coaches comment that "defence wins games." And great defence is based on attitude – an attitude that drives the defender to ensure that no ball hits the ground.

Defensive techniques include the ***simple dig***, the ***sprawl***, and the ***dive***. Most digs are made within a metre of the initial body position and primarily utilize the simple dig technique. This technique is similar to the volley pass or forearm pass, depending on whether the ball is contacted above or below the shoulders. The stance is wider, with overall posture lower to the ground.

Extended body techniques such as the sprawl and the dive involve the body making contact with the floor. They allow the defender to extend the range in which balls can be successfully retrieved. The proper application of these techniques ensures that the defender can play with seemingly reckless abandon with no fear of sustaining an injury.

Drills to develop the skill

D85 **Controlled pepper**   Player A stands with her back to the net. Player B is near the end line. Player A attacks the ball at player B, who digs the ball back to player A. Player A retrieves the ball and repeats.

D86 **Pepper**   Same as D85 but after player B digs the ball, player A volleys it back to player B. Player B attacks the ball at player A, who digs the ball back to player B. Player B volleys it back to player A, and the sequence repeats.

D87 **Setter's pepper**   Similar to D86 with the addition of a third player who is the designated setter. The ball is dug to the setter, who volleys it back to the digger to attack.

D88 **Three-player pepper**   Player A attacks the ball at players B and C, who are standing beside each other about 2 metres apart. The player that does not dig the ball will be the setter. This player must quickly run halfway toward player A, the original hitter, turn to face the digger (player B), and then volley the ball back to player B. The setter now runs backward and stands beside player A. Player B attacks the ball at players A and C. The player that does not dig the ball will be the setter. The sequence repeats.

DRILLS

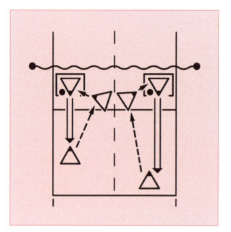

D89 **Basic digging**   Two players stand on a table (elevated) at opposite ends of the net in positions 4 and 2. Two players are in positions 5 and 1. The net players spike balls down the line at the backcourt players, who dig balls to a target in position 3.

Variations:

(a) Net players spike the ball cross-court at the backcourt players.

(b) Net players alternate spiking balls down the line and cross-court at the backcourt players.

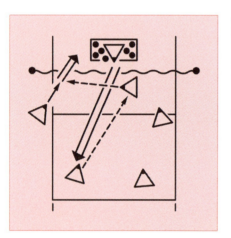

D90 **Dig to attack**   A player stands on a table (elevated) on the other side of the net and hits balls to players in position 5 or 1. A player located at the target area then sets players to attack from positions 2 or 4.

Variation: The attack is defended.

D91 **Digger's weave**   Players line up in positions 5 and 1. Coaches are hitters and targets located in positions 2 and 4. The coach in position 2 hits cross-court to player A in position 5. The ball is dug and player B in position 1 moves to volley the ball to the target in position 4. Players A and B switch lines. The coach in position 4 hits cross-court to player C in position 1. The ball is dug and player D in position 5 moves to volley the ball to the target in position 2. Players C and D switch lines. The sequence continues.

Variation: Additional players are in positions 4 and 2. They attack the set ball.

152

DIGGING

D92 Kojima   Three players are in positions 5, 6, and 1. The coach is at the net in position 3. The coach tosses/hits the ball at the players, and they must dig the ball back to the coach. The coach immediately tosses/hits the ball back at the players. When a ball is misplayed, the coach puts another ball into play.

Variation: <u>Setter's Kojima</u>   The players dig the ball, and a setter volleys the ball back to the coach to toss/hit at the players.

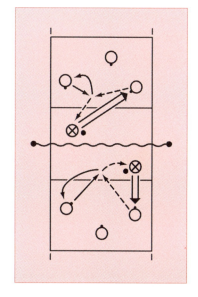

D93 Hitter's Kojima   Five players position themselves on the volleyball court as shown. Three players are in the backcourt and two players at the net – one in position 2 and the other in position 4. One of the players at the net attacks a ball at one of the four players, who must pass the ball up in the air for another player to pass the ball to one of the outside corner positions at the net. Players try to return to their initial starting positions as the player at the net who has been passed the play then continues to attack the ball. Players stay in the drill either for a certain time period or until they are able to consecutively dig and pass the ball up successfully a given number of times.

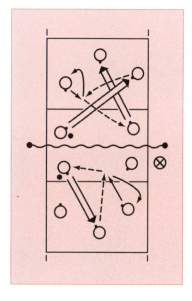

D94 Mini-games   Games of four-on-four or five-on-five (three backcourt players) where the ball is introduced in various ways. The ball can be introduced by the coach putting in a downball, hitting at a particular defender, or tossing for the ball to be attacked immediately.

DRILLS

Chart 4

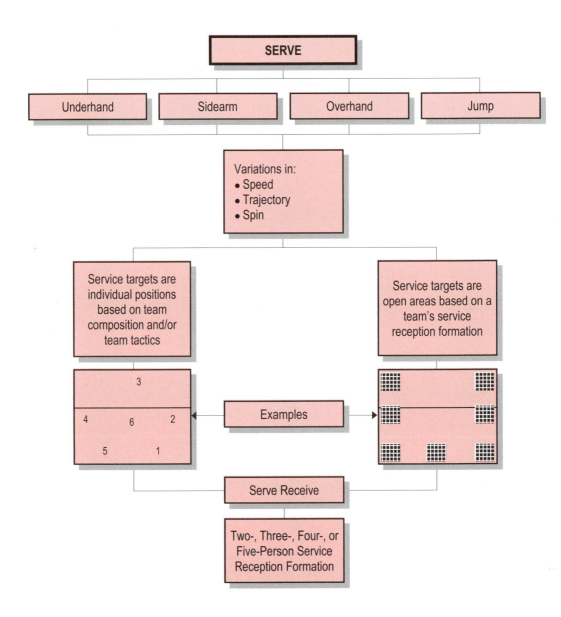

The serve

The serve is the skill that initiates play in the game of volleyball. Because it is the only skill where the athlete has full control of the ball, it is also a team's first chance at offence. Successful serves can minimize the effectiveness of the opponent's offence, thus enabling the serving team to more successfully defend their own court. At the younger levels, the serve may be the most important technical element that can determine the outcome of a match.

The serve is a throwing action. The action is a combination of lower body and upper body movements. The lower body movements involve a transfer of weight, while the upper body movements involve a swinging action by the hitting arm. The actions are similar in the underhand, sidearm, and overhand serve variations. The jump (spike) serve, as the name indicates, is similar to the spike.

The following are components of the *serve*:

- **Posture** – A cue word for the service posture is "*statue*." There are slight variations of the service posture depending on whether the athlete is executing an underhand, sidearm, overhand, or jump serve.

    In the *underhand service posture*, the player stands with feet together with the body facing the target. The ball is held in the nonhitting hand slightly ahead of the body at hip level.

    In the *sidearm service posture*, the player stands perpendicular to the target. Feet are together, and the volleyball is held in the nonhitting hand, with the arm straight ahead of the body and parallel to the floor. The hitting arm is parallel to the ground, making a 90-degree angle with the nonhitting arm.

    In the *overhand service posture*, the player stands perpendicular to the target. The arms make a "U" shape, with hands held high and elbows at eye level. The line joining the hands and head is directed toward the intended target.

- **Lower body movement** – The weight is transferred by taking a step with the foot on the side of the body opposite the hitting arm. This step is taken in the direction that the ball will be served.

- **Upper body movement** – With the underhand serve, the arm swings to hit the ball. With the sidearm and overhand serves, the body turns slightly to face the direction of the serve as the arm swings to contact the ball.

- **Ball toss** – With the underhand and sidearm serves, the holding hand is slightly dropped on contact with the striking arm. The overhand serve involves a vertical toss slightly ahead of the shoulder opposite the hitting hand.

- **Ball contact** – The hand can be open, with contact on the ball being made by the flat surface of the lower part of the palm (heel of the hand). Another technique is to make contact with the flat surface of a half-closed fist. To get a float action (knuckleball effect), the ball must be contacted at its midpoint in line with the centre of gravity.

DRILLS

> **Word cues and phrases for the serve include**
> 1. statue
> 2. underhand – step, swing, hit
>   sidearm – step, turn, swing, hit
>   overhand – toss, step, turn, swing, hit

In the overhand service posture, the elbow is held high and back, and the hand is held well above the head.

SERVE

Drills to develop the skill

D95 <u>Wall serve</u>   Players stand 5 metres away from a wall and serve against the wall.

D96 <u>Zone serve</u>   Lines are drawn parallel to the net at distances of 4, 5, 6, 7, and 8 metres. Each player begins in zone A (zone A is 3 to 4 metres from the net, zone B is 4 to 5 metres from the net, and so on). After a successful serve, players move to the next zone. Continue until players serve from the end line.

Variations:

(a) After a service error is made, the player must once again begin in zone A.

(b) Players start in the same zone on opposite sides of the net. The ball is served to a partner, who passes the ball to herself, then returns the serve.

D97 <u>Simple serving</u>   Players serve from the end line with a goal in mind. The following can be considered:

- Serve a given number of balls.
- Serve a given number of balls in a given time.
- Serve a given number of balls successfully.
- Serve a given number of balls successfully in succession. When an error is made, begin again.

D98 <u>Partner serve</u>   Partners serve the ball to each other from opposite end lines. Determine which pair has reached a target number of successful serves first.

Variation: Serves are executed from one side only. The ball is caught or received by the partner, then positions are switched.

D99 <u>Pressure</u>   The team lines up on one end line. The first player serves. If the serve is successful, the second player serves the next ball, and so on. If a service error is made, everyone must do a contingency (e.g., push-ups, line sprints). The drill then continues with the next player in line being the first server. The drill ends when everyone on the team has served successfully in order.

DRILLS

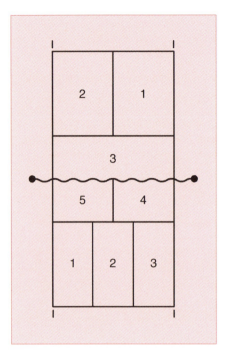

D100 Serving golf Section the court into areas as shown. Count the number of serves (strokes) it takes to successfully serve into an area. Move on to the next area (hole), and count the number of serves. The lowest score is the winner. Also see G32.

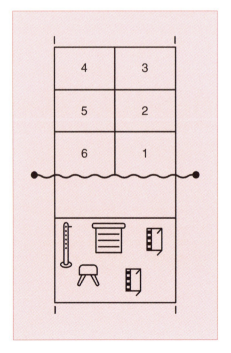

D101 Avoid the target Equipment is set up in the court, such as ball bins or box horses, to resemble an opponent's service reception formation. The players should serve to avoid hitting the objects.

Variation: Players must serve into designated areas marked on the court, trying to hit the marked areas in a numbered sequence.

SERVE

Service and service reception

D102a Three-player serve and receive
Three players (A, B, and C) begin on the court as outlined in the diagram. Player A serves the ball to player B. Player B passes the ball to player C (the target at the net). Player C tosses the ball back to player A. To increase contacts in less time, two balls can be utilized.

Variation: A second passer (D) is waiting at the sideline. After player B passes the ball, the target rates the pass as either a good pass or a poor pass. Player B goes to the sideline, and player D enters as the next passer. After player D passes the ball, the target rates the pass. Player D returns to the sideline and player B returns to pass. This continues until one passer reaches a goal of a given number of good passes.

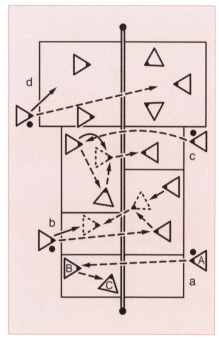

D102b Decide and move
Two passers stand 3 metres apart and 3 metres from the end line. The ball is served and a decision is made on who will pass the ball. The player who does not pass the ball runs to the target area at the net, catches the ball, and then returns it to the server.

Variation: Instead of the target catching the ball, the player sets the ball to the passer, who then volleys it back over the net for the next serve (D102c).

D102d Competition serve and receive
Similar to the drills above but players play out the rally to score points after each serve, three-on-three. The first team to score a certain amount of points is the winner.

DRILLS

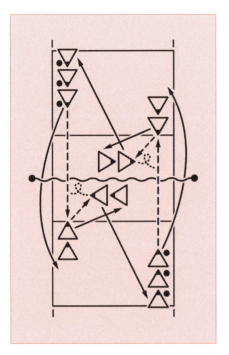

D103 **Butterfly or continuity serve and receive** After contacting the ball, players follow the path of the ball and go to the next area. The server goes to the passing line, the passer goes to the target line, and the target goes to the service line on the same side of the net. Targets pass to themselves before catching the ball and joining the end of the service line.

Variations:

(a) <u>Lengthwise half-court butterfly drill</u> Instead of the target going to the service line on the same side of the net, the target goes under the net to the end of the service line from where the ball originated.

(b) The target sets the passer, who attacks the ball down the line. The server attempts to dig the attack.

After the ball is passed on serve receive, players must prepare for the next phase of team play.

SERVE

There are risk and reward consequences associated with the difficulty of the jump serve. The greater the proficiency with the technique, the greater the reward.

DRILLS

Chart 5

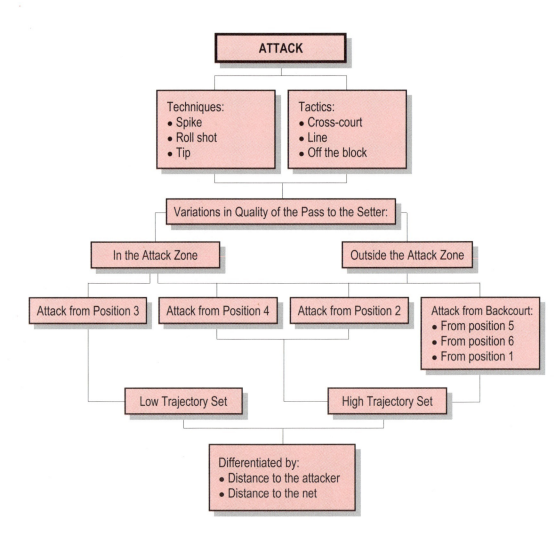

The attack

The attack is the culmination of a team's offence. A variety of attack techniques can be employed in a game. The spike is the one most utilized by players. The other techniques include the roll shot and the tip.

The dynamic nature of hitting a ball while in the air makes spiking one of the most difficult motor skills to master. It involves jumping maximally into the air to contact a ball that must clear a net and elude blockers and backcourt defenders in order to be successful. Spiking is one of the most exciting aspects of the game of volleyball, and that is perhaps why it is the skill players prefer to practice the most.

The spike is a throwing action with similarities to the serve. There is a rhythmic quality to the approach, jump, and landing components of the spike.

The following are components of the *spike*:

- **Footwork** – A three-step approach is used to prepare the attacker to jump into the air to contact the ball. For a right-handed attacker, the first step is with the left foot, followed very quickly by the right and left feet coming together. From both feet, the attacker jumps into the air. For a left-handed attacker the first step is with the right foot, followed by the left and then right.

- **Arm action** – In coordination with the footwork, both arms are swung back with the first step. They are then forcefully swung forward with the coming together of the feet and swung upward when jumping into the air. The arms continue the upward motion and swing into a "statue" position prior to contacting the ball. The arm swing can be described as a pendulum action.

- **Ball contact** – Action is similar to a throwing action. The nonhitting arm is brought down as the shoulders turn. The striking arm fully extends to contact the ball slightly ahead of the body with the open hand. The fingers are spread around the ball and, with a wrist snap, create topspin to drive the ball downward.

- **Follow-through** – After ball contact, the hitting arm swings forward and down, avoiding contact with the net. The landing should be balanced, preferably on two feet with knees bent to absorb impact.

Word cues and phrases for the spike include

1. pendulum swing to statue

2. left, right–left rhythm (for right-handed players; opposite for left-handed players)

3. gather momentum (swing down), transfer momentum (swing up), attack

DRILLS

Drills to develop the skill

D104 **Spike approaches**   Players stand at the attack line on either side of the net. They approach the net using the appropriate footwork and arm action. They return to the attack line and repeat.

D105 **Spike arm action**   Two players face each other as they stand at the attack line on either side of the net. Player A holds the ball with two hands and tosses it into the air. The player then continues to swing his arms into a "statue" position and then hits the ball over the net, utilizing the correct spike arm action. Player B catches the ball and returns it, utilizing the correct spike arm action.

Variation: Player B passes the spiked ball to herself, catches it, and then returns it, utilizing the correct spike arm action.

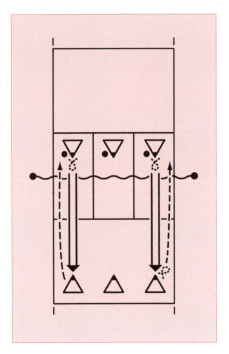

D106 **Toss and hit**   Two players face each other on either side of the net. Player A stands near the net, tosses the ball into the air, then jumps and hits the ball over the net toward player B, who is standing near the end line. Player B retrieves the ball and rolls it back under the net to player A. Repeat.

Variations:

(a)   Player B passes (digs) the ball to himself and then returns it to player A.

(b)   Player B passes (digs) to herself. She then goes to the net, tosses the ball, and hits it over the net to player A.

164

ATTACK

D107 **Spiking line** Half the players form hitting lines starting at the attack line in either position 4, 3, or 2. The other half of the players will shag balls and hand them to the coach. The coach stands at the net, 3 metres away from where the athlete will attack, and tosses balls for players to attack. After attacking, the player returns to the end of the hitting line. Hitting line and shaggers switch.

Variation: Attackers toss their balls to a setter, who volleys the ball (sets) to them. The setter can be in position 3 and volley the ball forward to position 4 or backward to position 2.

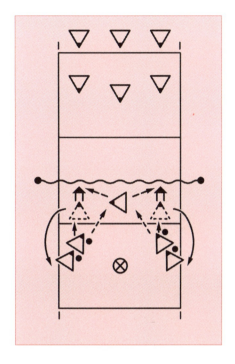

D108 **Pass and attack** The ball is tossed or served to the attacking player in position 5, who passes the ball to the target at the net. The target sets the ball high outside for the attack.

Variations:

(a) Target mats are placed in different areas for the attacker to hit.

(b) The coach calls out which target mat has to be hit just before the attacker jumps.

(c) A blocker at the net initiates the rally, and the attacker hits against the blocker.

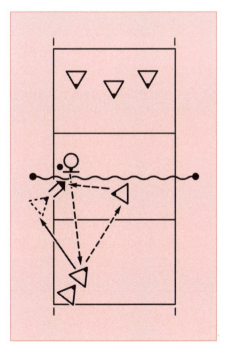

DRILLS

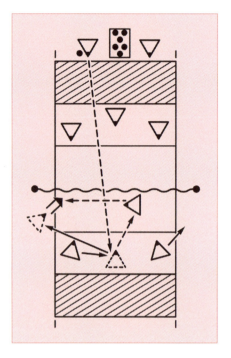

D109 Weave hitting Three players begin on a volleyball court as shown – a setter at the net in position 3 and two passers ready to receive the serve. The ball is served and a player passes it up to the setter. The two players at either sideline then prepare to attack. The setter volleys to either the player in position 4 or position 2 on either sideline, who attacks the ball. After the attack, the players realign such that the attacker and the middle player switch positions. The ball is served to begin the next repetition.

Variation: The court is shortened to emphasize control and placement.

Scoring variations:

- Drill ends after a given number of attack attempts
- Drill ends after a given number of successful attacks
- Drill ends after scoring a given number of points
    - 1 point for a successful attack
    - 0 points if the ball touches the net
    - −1 point if an attack error is made

D110 Weave hitting with blockers Similar to D109 with blockers added. Players on the attacking side focus on attack coverage.

Scoring variations:

- 1 point for a successful attack
- 0 points for a ball that is touched by the block and can be easily dug
- −1 point if the ball is blocked or an attack error is made

D111 Weave hitting versus defence Similar to D110 with backcourt players added.

Scoring variations:

- 1 point for a successful attack
- 0 points for a ball that is dug
- −1 point if the ball is blocked or an attack error is made

ATTACK

In the attack, the nonhitting arm is brought down as the shoulders turn. The striking arm fully extends to contact the ball slightly ahead of the body with the open hand.

DRILLS

Chart 6

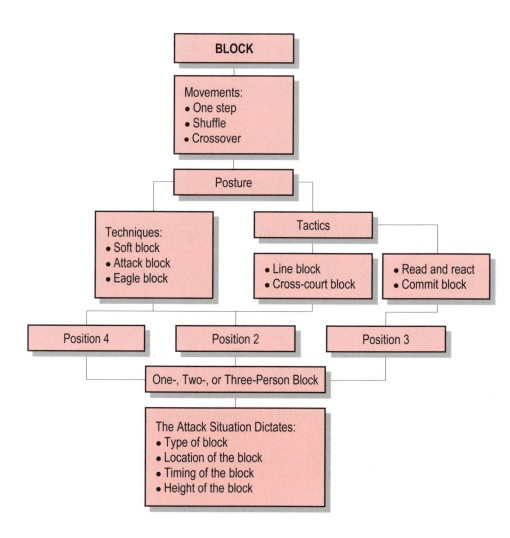

The block

The block is a team's first line of defence. For some, it is the primary defensive option; its purpose is to prevent the ball from crossing the net. For others, it is part of a defensive scheme that directs an opponent's attack toward backcourt defenders. Techniques include the attack block, soft block, or eagle block whether in a single-, double-, or triple-person block situation.

Blocking is the least important skill at beginning levels of play because ball control is inconsistent, and the potential for an opponent's powerful spike is erratic. As ability levels increase, knowing when to block or not to block becomes a critical decision.

Blocking is the most difficult volleyball skill to master. Although it occurs in most rallies, the number of situations where the block terminates the rally is minimal. Thus, players derive very little intrinsic positive feedback from executing technically correct blocks.

Most good blockers are tall with long arms and big hands, although short blockers can also be effective. Blockers must master the complex split-second evaluative processes and decision making involved in blocking. The height and speed of a set ball, how far off the net it is attacked, and the attacker's arm speed and swing style as well as jumping ability must be considered. In addition, movement ability, balance, and timing are fundamental traits of a good blocker.

The following are components of *blocking*:

- **Ready position** – Standing less than an arm's length away from the net, feet parallel to the net and shoulder-width apart. The knees are comfortably flexed, the back is straight, and hands are held above and slightly in front of the head. Arms are apart with fingers spread and stiff, palms facing the net. This is the "caribou" position.

- **Movement patterns** – Shuffle step, crossover step, turn and run.

- **Positioning** – Front the attacker to meet the ball crossing the net. The sequencing of information processing goes from watching the passed **ball** to the **setter**, the release of the **ball** from the setter's hands, the **attacker**, and then the attacked **ball**.

- **Blocking action** – The body dips, followed by a powerful extension of the hips, knees, and ankles. The arms are thrust upward and the hands thrust forward over the net.

DRILLS

> Word cues and phrases for the block include
>
> 1. caribou
> 2. ball, setter, ball, attacker, ball
> 3. delay (timing when jumping)

Drills to develop the skill

D112 Static blocking   A player begins at the net and assumes a proper blocking posture. A partner stands on a table (elevated) on the other side of the net and holds a ball above the net. The player jumps and presses his hands against the ball in an appropriate blocking action.

Variation: The partner holds two balls above the net. This reinforces the arm separation for the block.

D113 Simple blocking   A player begins at the net and assumes a proper blocking posture. A partner stands on the attack line on the opposite side of the net and tosses the ball slightly over the net. The blocker must jump and block the ball onto the tosser's side of the court.

Variation: The partner stands on a table (elevated) and tosses the ball high to herself, then spikes the ball into the blocker.

D114 Blocking with movement   Players begin in position 4 with good blocking posture and execute a block. They move laterally (shuffle step) at the net to position 3, where they execute another block. They continue to position 2, where they execute a third block. The next player in line begins when the preceding player is in position 3. The first player returns to the end of the line.

Variations:

(a) Players begin in position 2 and move to 3 and finish at 4.

(b) After finishing along one side of the net, players go to the opposite side of the net and continue movement in the opposite direction.

Chart 7

SUMMARY OF INDIVIDUAL TECHNIQUE AND TACTICS WITH THE BALL

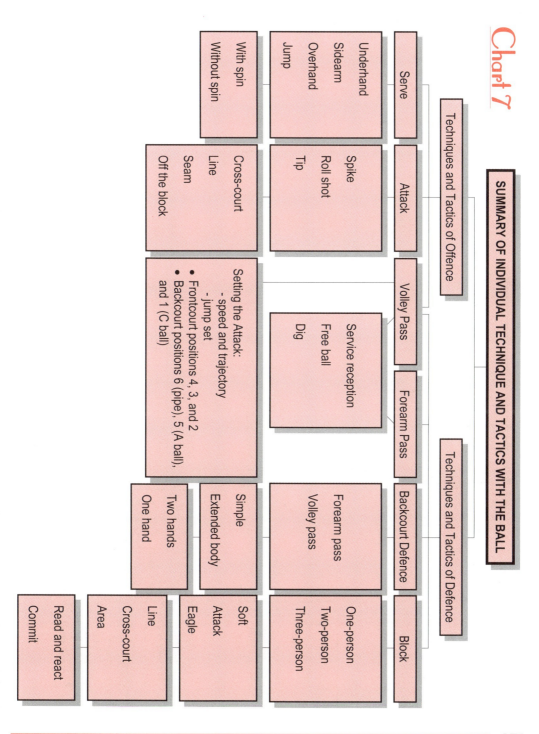

- Techniques and Tactics of Offence
  - Serve
    - Underhand
    - Sidearm
    - Overhand
    - Jump
    - With spin
    - Without spin
  - Attack
    - Spike
    - Roll shot
    - Tip
    - Cross-court
    - Line
    - Seam
    - Off the block
  - Volley Pass
    - Setting the Attack:
      - speed and trajectory
      - jump set
      - Frontcourt positions 4, 3, and 2
      - Backcourt positions 6 (pipe), 5 (A ball), and 1 (C ball)
  - Forearm Pass
    - Service reception
    - Free ball
    - Dig

- Techniques and Tactics of Defence
  - Backcourt Defence
    - Volley pass
    - Forearm pass
      - One-person
      - Two-person
      - Three-person
    - Simple
    - Extended body
      - Soft
      - Attack
      - Eagle
    - Two hands
    - One hand
      - Line
      - Cross-court
      - Area
  - Block
    - Read and react
    - Commit

BLOCK

DRILLS

Chart 8: TEAM PLAY

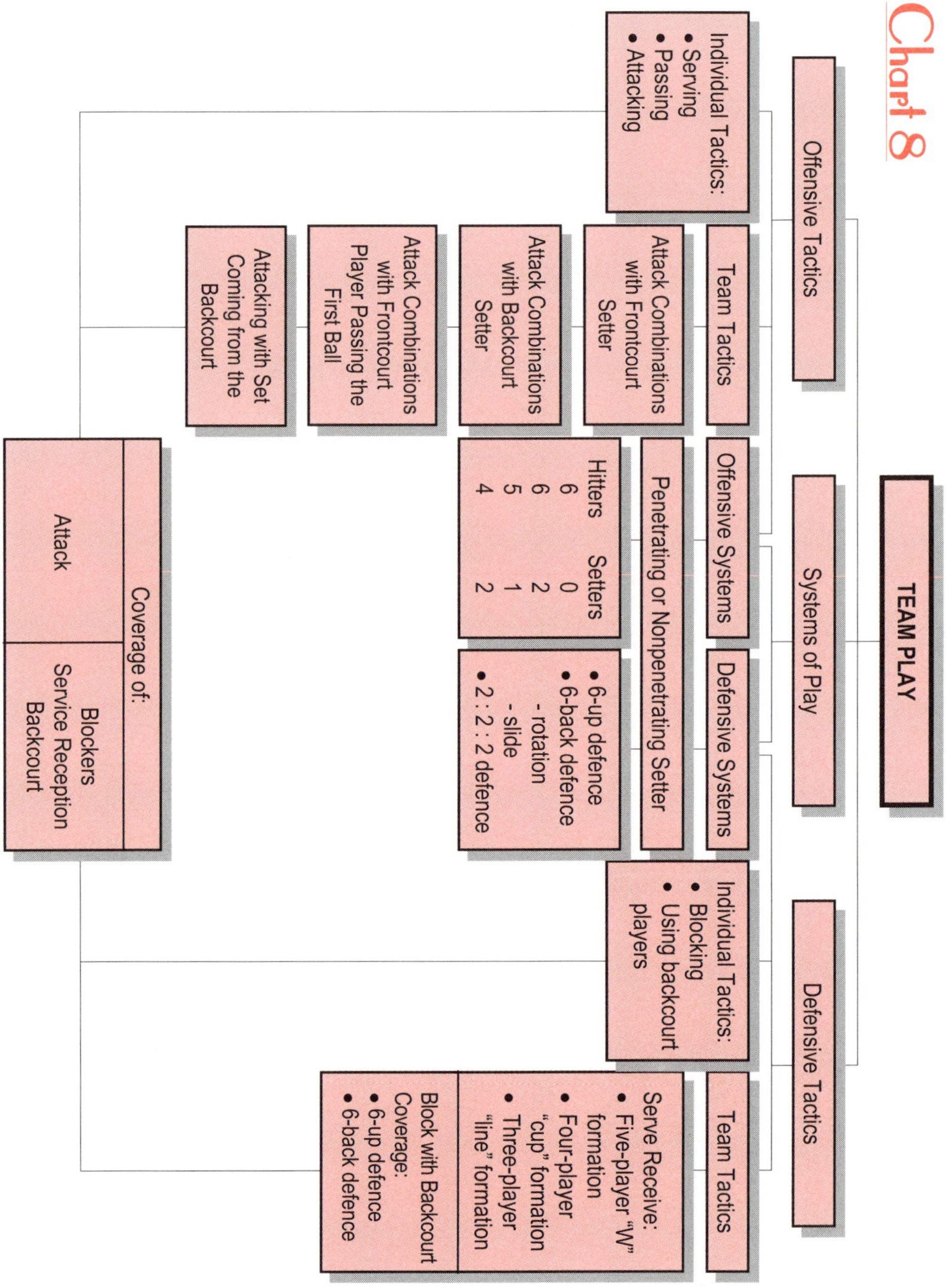

Offensive Tactics
- Individual Tactics:
  - Serving
  - Passing
  - Attacking
- Team Tactics:
  - Attack Combinations with Frontcourt Setter
  - Attack Combinations with Backcourt Setter
  - Attack Combinations with Frontcourt Player Passing the First Ball
  - Attacking with Set Coming from the Backcourt

Systems of Play
- Offensive Systems
  - Penetrating or Nonpenetrating Setter

Hitters	Setters
6	0
6	2
5	1
4	2

- Defensive Systems
  - 6-up defence
  - 6-back defence
    - rotation
    - slide
  - 2 : 2 : 2 defence

Defensive Tactics
- Individual Tactics:
  - Blocking
  - Using backcourt players
- Team Tactics:
  - Serve Receive:
    - Five-player "W" formation
    - Four-player "cup" formation
    - Three-player "line" formation
  - Block with Backcourt Coverage:
    - 6-up defence
    - 6-back defence
  - Coverage of:
    - Blockers
    - Service Reception
    - Backcourt Attack

172

Team play

The major characteristic of play in any team sport is the continuous integration of basic skills in a succession of rapidly changing situations. Play is not a series of isolated skills strung together but rather a series of phases where the players are continually confronted with differing responsibilities. In addition, instantaneous tactical decisions need to be made in order to successfully execute various tasks.

Players need to be good at reading cues and anticipating the actions of their opponents. Minimizing time spent in drills that isolate the basic skills and spending more time in "real game situations" will accelerate a player's ability to identify situations. This in turn will result in better decision making and more effective execution of tactical strategies.

Following are guidelines to be considered in order to effectively develop and organize *team play* drills:

- **Isolate game situations** – Drills should be based on simplified rally situations. Players must execute appropriate techniques and tactics in these situations.

- **Focus the drill** – The content of the drill should incorporate at least one primary action or situation related to the rally. Supporting actions and movements should not be neglected or ignored.

- **Respect positional relationships** – Proper court positioning is maintained by players with respect to each other, the net, and boundary lines of the court.

- **Rally out** – In the drill, the primary action may be preceded and should be followed by play corresponding to the rally situation. Artificially ending a rally may decrease the drill's learning outcomes.

- **Control speed and tempo** – The speed and tempo of play should mimic game situations. However, the dynamics of the rally can be increased by manipulating its intensity. This is accomplished by minimizing the rest before the commencement of the next sequence or rally.

- **Practice player dynamics** – The drill should be arranged so that the cooperation and shared responsibilities between and among players is consistent with what is desired in the actual game. This is especially important for avoiding misunderstandings in situations such as coverage assignments.

- **Include an opponent** – Opponents are included in order to influence demands of play. The actions of an opponent affect tactical decision making.

- **Include measurable results** – The drill should contain a measurable objective that clearly indicates the effectiveness of execution. Manipulating scoring outcomes can increase motivation.

DRILLS

Setting up the drills

Players involved

Team play drills need not be scrimmages where players are organized to compete in typical six-on-six game situations. Team play drills can use any combination of players, including the following:

- Four-on-four
- Four-on-five (three frontcourt players)
- Four-on-five (three backcourt players)
- Four-on-six
- Five-on-five (three frontcourt players)
- Five-on-five (three backcourt players)
- Five-on-five (three frontcourt versus three backcourt players)
- Five-on-six (three frontcourt players)
- Five-on-six (three backcourt players)
- Six-on-six

(See Part III, "How to Play the Game," for formations and player responsibilities.)

Initiation of rallies

Team play drills basically involve rally sequences. The rally sequences in these drills can be initiated in a number of different ways: by a coach, by an extra player, or even by a player on the playing court. The introduction of the ball into the rallies can be by served balls, downballs, free balls, tossed balls, spiked balls, and so on.

Initiation skill followed by tactical response

The drill can be initiated with a specific skill or player focus that will be followed by a tactical response (Table 5.1).

Table 5.1 Initiation skill followed by tactical response.

INITIATION SKILL	TACTICAL RESPONSE
Serve	Service reception to attack
Serve reception	Setting up the attack
Dig	Transition to attack
Set	Attack
Attack	Defence
Block	Attack coverage

Scoring

Scoring in team play drills can modify the focus of the game, redesign tactics, and effectively alter the mental and physical aspects of the workout. Examples of scoring systems follow:

Regular scoring – A point is awarded to the side that wins the rally.

Earned point versus unearned point scoring – A point is awarded to the side that wins the rally only if it is an earned point. An earned point is one in which the rally ends based on a positive action (i.e., a successful attack, a successful block, an ace serve). An unearned point is one in which the rally ends because of an unforced error (i.e., a misplayed ball, an attacked ball that goes out of bounds, a line violation).

Variation: A point is awarded to the side that wins the rally on earned points only. A point is subtracted from the side that loses the rally based on an unearned point.

Wash scoring – Two or more rallies must be won in order to score a point. If a team cannot fulfill the scoring requirements, then a "wash" is declared and no points are scored. The team play drill is over when a predetermined number of points are scored. As an example, side A begins a serve rally, while side B begins a downball rally. The ball is served to side A and the rally is played out. As soon as the rally ends, side B receives a downball and the rally is played out. If one side wins both rallies it scores a point. If each side wins a rally then a "wash" is declared and no points are scored.

Handicap scoring – In general, a team on offence (in control of the ball) has an advantage over the defending team. Also the starting (more skilled) players on a team should have an advantage over the substitute (less skilled) players. In these situations, a

DRILLS

handicap scoring system can be implemented to try to even out the competition and provide more incentive to execute properly.

In the situation of offence versus defence a handicap scoring system could have the team that initiates the first offensive sequence score 1 point if it wins the rally and the other team score 2 points if it wins the rally. Similarly, in a first team (starters) versus second team (substitutes) scenario, the first team scores 1 point if it wins the rally and the second team scores 2 points if it wins the rally.

End game scoring – In this situation, the team play drill begins with a score that is near the end of a set (e.g., 23–20). The drill is played out until a winner is declared (set to 25 points with a minimum 2-point advantage).

Side to initiate rally

Drill dynamics, especially psychological aspects, can change dramatically depending on which side initiates the rally. There are three scenarios that determine which side will initiate the rally.

The ball is introduced to alternating sides – There is no additional consequence to winning or losing the rally. Each side will thus get equal opportunities to execute the skills and work on appropriate tactical responses. Consideration may be given to include a handicap scoring system. The side on which the ball is introduced would score 1 point for winning the rally, while the other side would score 2 points for winning the rally.

The ball is introduced to the side that loses the rally – This is typical of regular game situations. The losing side must be successful and immediately gets another opportunity to make adjustments and execute appropriately in order to become successful.

The ball is introduced to the side that wins the rally – In this scenario, the psychological dynamics can become very interesting. The side on which the ball is introduced may be at an advantage, particularly if the players can control the ball immediately. The side can develop momentum where it can win a number of consecutive rallies. It can be motivating for those players and very frustrating for the opposing side.

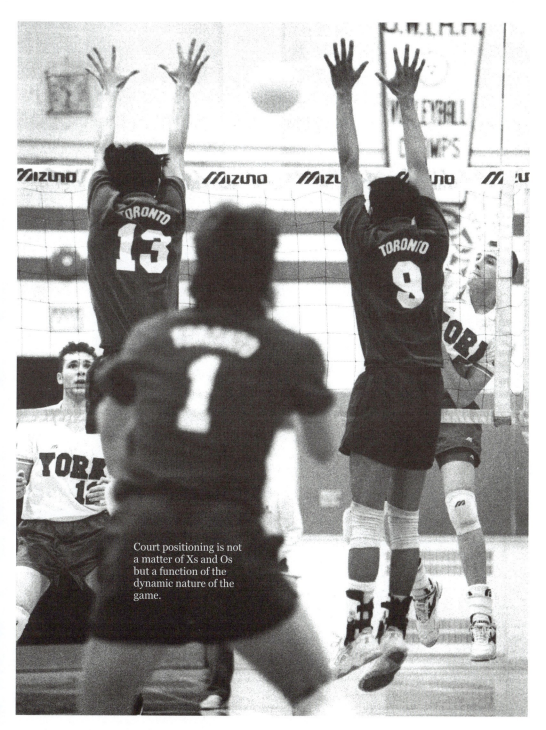

TEAM PLAY

Court positioning is not a matter of Xs and Os but a function of the dynamic nature of the game.

DRILLS

Drills to develop the skill

Team play focus — Service

D115 Teams A and B, of equal ability, will be made up of four players each (four-on-four), with the remaining four players (R, S, T, and U) divided between the two teams. Players R and S will serve for team A. Players T and U will serve for team B. They will be the only players serving.

Teams will use the line service reception formation and employ the four-on-four team play situations as outlined in Part III, "How to Play the Game." Teams will alternate service after every rally.

- The team that wins the rally scores 1 point.
- An ace serve scores 2 points.
- The receiving team scores 2 points on a service error.

Variations:

(a) The team that wins the rally continues to serve with the same server.

(b) If there is a service error, the server must do a contingency (e.g., five push-ups, five extended body digs).

D116 The first team (starting lineup) will receive the ball and play against the second team (substitutes). One player from the first team is substituted. This player is the designated server for the second team, who will serve until the first team has successfully sided out (won the rally) in each of the six service reception rotations. The total points scored by the second team are recorded.

The drill is repeated until all members of the first team have been the designated server for the second team.

The competition in the drill is among the servers. The best server designation would go to the individual who served during the drill in which the second team scored the most points.

Team play focus – Service reception to attack

D117 The first team will play against the second team (six-on-six). The first team will always receive the serve. Players will rotate accordingly and begin in proper service reception formations.

The second team will always serve. For this drill, the second team is not required to obey the overlap rule and to rotate positions. The coach may align players in certain positions in order to make the team more effective or to accustom the team to the process of switching. The server will be changed whenever the first team wins the rally. A service error is replayed with no team scoring a point.

If the first team wins the rally, it will score 1 point and rotate one position. If it loses the rally, players will stay in the same service reception formation. The second team will score a point.

The drill is over when the first team has successfully sided out (won the rally) in each of the six service reception rotations.

The calibre of play will dictate what the scoring goal of the drill should be. With novice players (age 14 and under) a realistic goal may be to win one of every three service rallies. Thus a scoring goal would be 6 points for the first team and 12 points for the second team. Elite college and university teams are capable of winning at least two out of every three service rallies. Thus a scoring goal would be 6 points for the first team and 3 points for the second team.

The coach should set the appropriate scoring goals. If goals are met, a reward may be given. If they are not met, then a contingency can be implemented.

D118 Similar to drill **D117**, but the focus is on one particular service reception formation. The first team must win a designated number of service reception rallies in order to rotate or get out of the drill. The server is changed after the receiving team wins a rally.

Variations:

(a) The receiving team has a maximum of X serves in order to win Y rallies. If the team is not successful, then the drill begins again.

(b) The receiving team must win X number of rallies consecutively. If the team loses a rally, the count begins again.

DRILLS

Team play focus – Dig to transition

D119 Teams A and B, of equal ability, will be made up of five players each (five-on-five – two frontcourt players in positions 4 and 2 and three backcourt players). The remaining players are shaggers. Both teams begin in initial defensive positions (see Part III, "How to Play the Game").

Two coaches (A and B) are positioned outside the left sideline of the court (at the midpoint between the net and the end line and 2 metres from the sideline). Coach A will hit downballs over the net to team A, while coach B will hit downballs over the net to team B.

The coach delivering the downball will give a signal and then toss the ball and hit it over the net. The team receiving the downball will make their appropriate defensive movements as if defending an attack from position 4. The rally is initiated and played out. At the completion of the rally, teams return to their initial defensive positions, and the other coach gives a signal before tossing the ball and hitting it over the net. Coaches will alternate delivering balls and have the option of hitting the downball to any position.

The team that wins the rally scores a point. The drill is played to 25 points with a 2-point margin.

Variations:

(a) The team that loses the rally gets the next downball.

(b) The team that wins the rally gets the next downball.

(c) Only earned points are counted.

(d) After 20 points, a team committing an unforced error loses a point.

(e) Can be set up for four-on-four or six-on-six.

D120 Similar to D119 except that coaches stand near the net on the same side of the court that they will input the ball. The coach delivering the ball will give a signal and then toss the ball and attack it at a particular position. The team receiving the ball will make their appropriate defensive movements as if defending an attack from position 4. The rally is initiated and played out. At the completion of the rally, teams return to their initial defensive positions, and the other coach gives a signal before tossing the ball and attacking it at a particular position. Coaches will alternate delivering balls and have the option of attacking the ball to any position.

TEAM PLAY

The team that wins the rally scores a point. The drill is played to 25 points with a 2-point margin.

Variations:

(a) The coach attacks the ball to a particular position to begin the rally.

(b) The team that loses the rally gets the next attacked ball.

(c) The team that wins the rally gets the next attacked ball.

(d) Only earned points are counted.

(e) After 20 points, a team committing an unforced error loses a point.

(f) Can be set up for four-on-four or six-on-six.

Team play focus — Setting to attack

D121 Teams A and B, of equal ability, will be made up of six players each. Both teams begin in their initial defensive positions (see Part III, "How to Play the Game"). The coach is positioned outside the end line of the court at the midpoint between the sidelines on the side that team A occupies. The coach gives a signal, which initiates preparatory attack movements by team A. The coach tosses the ball to a predetermined target area (ideal first contact pass), from where the designated setter sets the attack. The setter makes the decision on whom to set.

The team that wins the rally scores a point. The drill is played to 25 points with a 2-point margin.

Variations:

(a) The set from the coach's toss is predetermined before the rally begins.

(b) The coach tosses the ball to other predetermined targets on the court.

(c) The coach tosses the ball to random targets on the court.

(d) The coach is positioned outside the left sideline of the court across the net from team A (at the midpoint between the net and the end line and 2 metres from the sideline). After a signal, the coach delivers the ball (either a free ball or a downball) across the net. The setter tracks the ball and then makes an appropriate setting decision.

DRILLS

Team play focus — Attack

D122 Team A has four players and team B has six players (four-on-six). Team A begins in line service reception formation, and team B begins in initial defence (see Part III, "How to Play the Game"). The coach is positioned outside the end line of the court at the midpoint between the sidelines on the side that team A occupies. The coach gives a signal, which initiates preparatory attack movements by team A. The coach tosses the ball to a predetermined target area. The ball is set to position 4 and is attacked.

The drill begins at 20–20 and is played to 25 points with a 2-point margin.

Variations:

(a) The ball is set to position 2 and attacked.

(b) The coach stands on the opposite side of the net from team A. He delivers a served ball.

(c) Team A begins in initial defensive positions. The coach stands near the net on the same side of the court as team A. The coach will give a signal and then toss the ball and attack it to position 4. The ball is dug and set to position 4.

(d) Can be set up for five-on-six or six-on-six.

D123 Teams A and B, of equal ability, will be made up of five (two frontcourt – positions 2 and 4 – and three backcourt) players each. Team A begins in cup service reception formation, and team B begins in initial defence (see Part III, "How to Play the Game"). Remaining players are shaggers and servers.

The ball is served to team A and must be set to position 4 from service reception only. For the next rally, team A is in initial defence, and team B is in cup service reception formation. The ball is served to team B and again must be set to position 4 from service reception only.

The primary competition in this drill is between position 4 hitters. The game is played to 15 points with a 2-point margin.

Variations:

(a) Both teams begin in initial defensive positions, with the rally initiated by the coach delivering a downball or an attacked ball.

(b) The first attack in the rally must be from position 2.

TEAM PLAY

(c) Teams play six-on-six. Both teams begin in initial defensive positions, with the rally initiated by the coach delivering a free ball. The team winning the rally gets the free ball. The team winning the rally scores a point only if a designated player attacks the ball successfully to win the rally (e.g., middle attacker versus middle attacker).

The quality of execution in all aspects of team play is a critical determinant of a team's success.

Team play focus — Block and coverage

D124 Teams A and B, of equal ability, will be made up of five (three frontcourt and two backcourt – positions 5 and 1) players each. Team A will be in their defensive positions, defending an attack from position 4. Team B will be in their coverage positions as if attacking from position 4 (see "How to Play the Game"). The coach will be in position 4 on the side of the court occupied by team B. On the signal the coach tosses the ball and hits it into the two-person block formed by team A. This initiates the rally. Five repetitions are performed and then the roles of team A and team B are reversed.

Variations:

(a) The coach is in position 2 to initiate the rally.

(b) A predetermined attacker attempting to hit the ball into the block initiates the rally. Regardless of whether the ball is blocked, the rally is played out.

PART VI

CIRCUIT 1 *186*

CIRCUIT 2 *188*

CIRCUIT 3 *190*

CIRCUIT 4 *192*

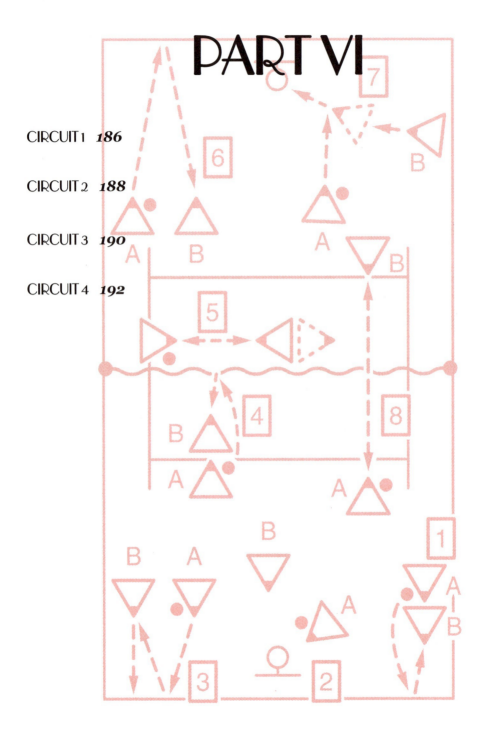

CIRCUIT TRAINING

Volleyball has evolved from a sport where technical skill was the primary key to success into a sport where at the highest levels well-developed physical abilities are paramount. One such method of developing these physical requirements is through circuit training.

Circuit training consists of a number of "stations" where the athlete performs a given exercise, usually within a specified time period. Once the exercise is completed at one station, the athlete immediately moves on to the next station, performing another exercise, also within a prescribed time period. The circuit is completed once the athlete performs the exercises at all stations.

The selection of exercises, time spent at each station, number of stations per circuit, and so on can be adapted to the athlete's age, training experience, and performance ability. The design of the circuit thus can focus on various levels of an athlete's training requirements. The requirements can range from endurance (aerobic, anaerobic, muscular) to strength, power, flexibility, and even technical skill development.

Circuit training has many valuable organizational aspects. It can accommodate a relatively large number of athletes at one time, requires relatively inexpensive equipment, and can be easily adapted to individual needs and abilities. Circuits should consist of between 6 and 15 stations, requiring a total time of between 5 and 20 minutes to complete. Usually, each circuit is performed several times in one training session. Rest periods between stations can range up to 30 seconds.

Several forms of circuit training exist, depending on the goals to be achieved in training. Two different forms of circuit training are presented in this section. For more information on circuit training, refer to *Circuit Training for All Sports*, a Sport Books Publisher publication.

CIRCUIT TRAINING

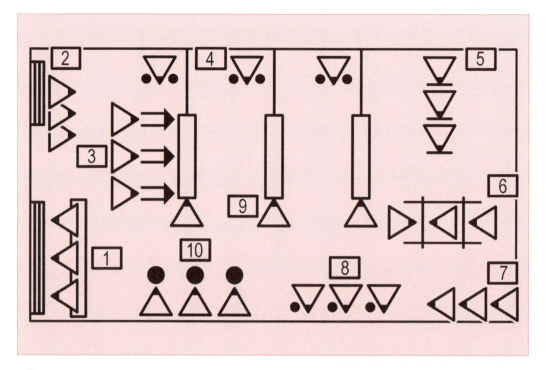

Circuit 1

Goal: To develop physical abilities, especially strength endurance and flexibility. Endurance can be especially important for five-set matches and tournaments.

Participants: The circuit can accommodate 10 to 30 players, with a maximum of 3 per station.

Expectations: The circuit is completed two or three times. The exercises are performed as efficiently as possible, keeping in mind quality of execution at the different stations. Players will work for 30 seconds then take a 30-second rest while moving to the next station.

Materials: Benches, bars or hockey sticks, dumbbells (5 kilograms), tennis balls, medicine balls (3 kilograms), parallel bars, shadows (inner tire tubes filled with sand to a weight of 5 to 10 kilograms), bench, wall ladder.

Circuit stations

Station 1:
Players sit on a bench facing a wall, which is 1 metre away. A minimum block jump height is marked. After a block jump, the players sit back on the bench.

CIRCUITS

Station 2:
Players assume a squat position, with their backs to a wall ladder. They reach behind and hold the wall ladder with hands at head height. The players then push themselves upward and forward, holding on to the wall ladder, then return to the squat position.

Station 3:
Benches are set up 3 metres apart. Players use a standing two-foot jump to clear each bench.

Station 4:
Players sit on the ground with a tennis ball in each hand. Balls are repeatedly squeezed in each hand.

Station 5:
Holding on to a hockey stick with arms fully extended, players jump over the stick with both feet. Players jump over forward and backward. Exercise caution.

Station 6:
Players perform body dips on parallel bars.

Station 7:
Players perform one-leg squats (using wall if support is needed), alternating legs with each repetition.

Station 8:
Players lie on their stomachs, 1 metre away from a wall, with shoulders parallel to the wall. They throw a medicine ball against the wall, alternating the throwing arm.

Station 9:
Players straddle a bench, which is 25-35 centimeters high. They jump onto the bench and then back to the original position. They can hold dumbbells in each hand or have a shadow on their shoulders for added resistance.

Station 10:
Players assume a squat position with a medicine ball held in both hands. The players rise and toss the medicine ball backward, over their heads against the wall. The players quickly turn and try to catch the medicine ball.

CIRCUIT TRAINING

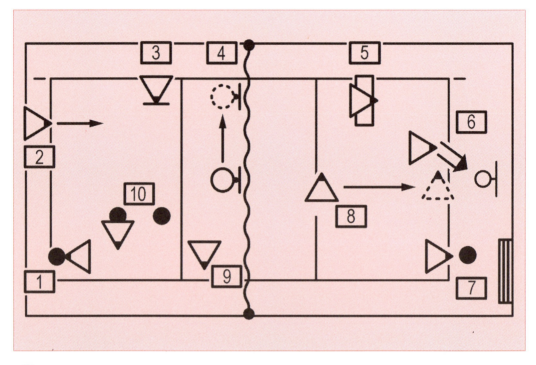

Circuit 2

Goal: To develop physical abilities, especially strength endurance and flexibility. Some of these exercises involve specific volleyball-related techniques.

Participants: The circuit can accommodate a maximum of 20 players, with a maximum of 2 per station.

Expectations: The circuit is completed two or three times. The exercises are performed as efficiently as possible, keeping in mind quality of execution at the different stations. One player will work for 15 seconds, then there will be a 15-second transition period. The second player will work for 15 seconds, followed by another 15-second transition period as the pair moves to the next station.

Materials: Bars or hockey sticks, medicine balls (2 or 3 kilograms), fitness board, volleyball court with net, basketball backboard and hoop.

Circuit stations

Station 1:
Players stand a distance of 2 metres from a wall. They chest pass the medicine ball against the wall, catching the rebound.

CIRCUITS

Station 2:
Players begin at the end line of a volleyball court. They run as fast as possible 9 metres to the net, run backward 3 metres to the attack line, 3 metres forward to the net, and then backward 9 metres to the end line. Repeat until time expires.

Station 3:
Players hold a bar in front of themselves, with hands approximately 1 metre apart. Holding on to the bar, they slowly move the bar above the head and behind the back, then return to the original position. Repeat.

Station 4:
Beginning at the middle of the net, players perform a block jump, then utilize appropriate footwork to run 4.5 metres to the sideline, execute a block jump, return to the middle of the net, and execute another block jump. Repeat.

Station 5:
Standing on the edge of a fitness board, keeping the knees straight, players flex forward at the hips, attempting to have fingertips go as far below the feet as possible. Hold for the full duration.

Station 6:
Players perform spike jump approach footwork with a spike jump, attempting to touch (above) the basketball rim. Repeat as often as possible.

Station 7:
Players perform deep squats with a medicine ball throw. Starting from a squatting position, players hold a medicine ball in front of the body with arms fully extended. As quickly as possible, they extend the legs and toss the medicine ball as high as possible against the wall.

Station 8:
Beginning at the attack line, players utilize a shuffle step, move sideways 6 metres to the end line, then return. Repeat as quickly as possible.

Station 9:
Players do push-ups, clapping hands between repetitions. A forceful extension phase is needed to provide sufficient time to clap hands and then place hands on the floor in the recovery phase.

Station 10:
Two medicine balls are placed on the court surface 3 metres apart. The players begin sitting on one ball, run to the other ball, sit down, then return to the first ball. Repeat.

CIRCUIT TRAINING

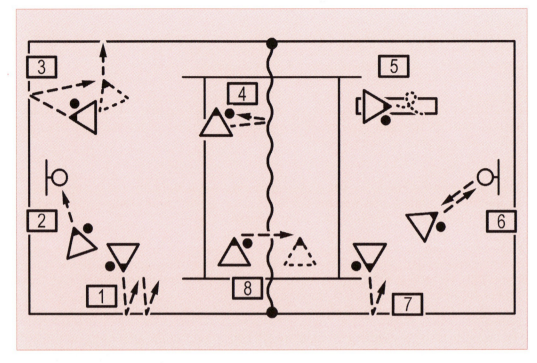

Circuit 3

Goal: To improve proficiency in the technical skills of the volley pass and the forearm pass.

Participants: The circuit can accommodate 8 to 16 players. Each station can have either one or two players working simultaneously.

Expectations: A time of 45 seconds is allocated for each station, with a 15-second transition and orientation period between stations. Each player works as effectively as possible within his or her own ability levels to maximize contacts and ball control. If necessary, short 1-minute breaks can be taken to review correct technique execution.

Materials: Volleyball court with net, two basketball backboards and hoops, bench, one volleyball per player.

Circuit stations

Station 1:
Standing 1 metre from a wall, players volley pass against the wall. Players can remain stationary or perform side movements, avoiding obstacles where necessary.

Station 2:
Players bounce the ball on the floor, then forearm pass the ball into a basketball hoop.

Station 3:
Players stand in the corner of the gymnasium, approximately 1 metre from the side and end walls. The players volley pass the ball against the wall, alternating each pass between the side and end walls. Players turn their bodies after each pass, ensuring that the full body posture faces the appropriate target wall.

Station 4:
Players stand perpendicular to the net, approximately 1.5 to 3 metres away from the net. The players toss the ball into the lower portion of the net, then take appropriate action to forearm pass the ball straight up into the air. Players catch the ball and repeat.

Station 5:
Players repeatedly volley pass to themselves while walking back and forth over a bench.

Station 6:
Players underhand toss the ball against a basketball backboard, then forearm pass the ball into the basketball hoop.

Station 7:
A target circle is drawn on a wall, with the centre of the circle approximately 3 metres above the ground. Players volley pass the ball at the circle, forearm pass the returning ball to themselves, and then volley pass back at the circle.

Station 8:
Players stand perpendicular to the net. They pass the ball repeatedly over the net while going back and forth under the net. Choice of pass is determined by the coach or left to the discretion of each player.

CIRCUIT TRAINING

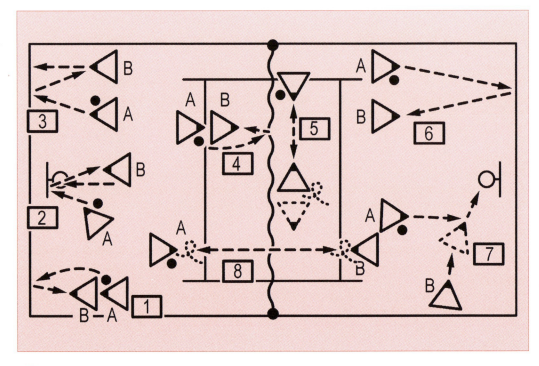

Circuit 4

Goal: To improve technical proficiency and accuracy of passing with a partner.

Participants: The circuit can accommodate 16 players. Each station must have players working as a pair.

Expectations: A time of 2 minutes is allocated for each station, which includes transitions between players and stations.

Materials: Volleyball court with net, two basketball backboards and hoops, one volleyball per station.

Circuit stations

Station 1:
Two players stand one in front of the other about 3 to 4 metres away from a wall. Player A throws the ball against the wall. Player B forearm passes the ball to herself, then volley passes the ball back to player A. Player B can use either a front volley pass or a back volley pass when passing the ball back to player A.

CIRCUITS

Station 2:
Player A tosses the ball against a basketball backboard. Player B receives the ball and uses either a volley pass or a forearm pass to attempt to put the ball into the basketball hoop. Players switch roles if the passed ball does not go into the basketball hoop.

Station 3:
Player A spikes the ball to the ground so that it rebounds off the wall. Player B then does the same with the rebounded ball. Players continue to alternate spiking the ball to the ground so that it rebounds off the wall.

Station 4:
Player A tosses the ball into the lower portion of the net. Player B runs to the net and forearm passes the ball back to player A.

Station 5:
Player A begins in position 2 and player B begins in position 3. Player A volley passes the ball to player B, who volley passes to himself, turns 180 degrees, then back volleys the ball to player A.

Station 6:
Player A and player B alternately volley pass the ball against the wall. After 1 minute the exercise is repeated with the forearm pass.

Station 7:
Player A volleys the ball to a target approximately 4 metres from a basketball hoop. Player B runs to the target area and volley passes the ball to the basketball hoop. After 1 minute, roles are switched.

Station 8:
Player A and player B stand on the attack line on either side of the volleyball net. Player A forearm passes to herself then volley passes to player B, who does the same.

LEAD-UP GAMES AND DRILLS

PART VII: GLOSSARY

Ace A serve that hits the floor or causes the serve receiver to misplay the ball to the extent that the ball cannot be controlled or returned to the opponent's side of the court.

Antennae Two thin, flexible striped rods that extend 80 centimetres above the net and are attached to the net at a distance of 9 metres from each other. Each antenna is directly over the sideline.

Attack The culmination of offence. The contact of the ball, above the height of the net, to direct it over the net with the intent of putting the ball on the opponent's court.

Attack block A block in which the blocker or blockers reach over the net and intercept the ball before it crosses the net, directing it back down into the opponent's court. Also known as a stuff block.

Attack coverage Nonattacking players back up the attacker by positioning themselves behind and close to the attacker in case the ball rebounds back into their court off of the defending team's block.

Attack line A line 3 metres from and parallel to the centre line.

Attack ready position The position on the court the attacker goes to in preparation to make an approach before attacking the ball.

Attack zone The area between the attack line and the centre line. A backcourt player cannot legally attack the ball if the last floor contact was in the attack zone.

Attacker A player who contacts the ball above the height of the net and directs the ball over the net with the intent of terminating the rally in his or her team's favour.

Back row See backcourt.

Back set A volley pass in which the ball is directed backward. In most instances the back set is directed to an attacker in position 2.

Backcourt The three positions on the court that are closest to the end line – positions 1, 6, and 5.

Backcourt player Any player in position 1, 6, or 5 at the time of service.

Backcourt set A volley pass that is directed to a backcourt player, who will attack the ball.

GLOSSARY

Ball handling — The manner in which the ball is contacted during a pass.

Basic volleyball play — The ideal elementary tactic where the ball is contacted three times on a side. On the first contact, the ball should be directed to the middle front of the net; on the second contact, the ball should be directed to a corner of the court at the net; and on the third contact, the ball should be directed over the net.

Block — A basic skill in which one or more frontcourt players prevent or attempt to prevent an opposition's attack from crossing the net.

Bump — See forearm pass.

Centre line — The line directly underneath the net that divides the playing area into two equal courts.

Coach-oriented drill — A drill in which the coach is actively involved. The coach initiates the action and thus controls the intensity, difficulty, and purpose of the drill.

Collapse — A defensive posture in which a player sits over one heel while playing a ball and then rolls onto his or her back. It is used to play balls that are close to the floor and to cushion hard spikes during retrieval attempts.

Cross-court block — A block in which the blockers attempt to prevent the attacker from directing the ball toward the far sideline of the court.

Cross-court spike — A spike that is directed diagonally toward the far sideline of the defending team's court.

Crossover step — A method of movement in which the player's lead foot is extended in the direction of movement and the trailing foot is brought up to and in front of the lead foot. This technique enables the player to shift while remaining square to the play.

Cup formation — A four-person service reception formation in which the team receiving the serve align themselves in a formation that resembles the outline of a cup.

Defence — Actions (techniques, tactics, and strategies) that are utilized with the purpose of preventing the ball from contacting the court.

Defensive system — A team tactical system of deploying players to specific positions in order to effectively defend an opponent's attack.

Dig — The act of successfully defending an attacked ball.

Digger — A player who attempts to dig a ball.

LEAD-UP GAMES AND DRILLS

Dive — An extended body technique in which a player extends for a ball near the floor, causing both feet to leave the ground. The player contacts the ball while in the air with one or both arms and then slides on the chest, abdomen, and thighs.

Downball — A situation in which an attack is relatively weak and the defence tries to field it with its backcourt players only.

End line — The boundary line at each end of the court.

Float serve — A serve in which the ball is contacted in such a manner that the ball has no spin, causing an unpredictable flight path (similar to a knuckle ball in baseball).

Foot fault — Stepping on or over the end line while serving, or any other active player standing outside the court at the time of service, or the complete crossing of the centre line during a rally.

Forearm pass — A ball-handling skill a player uses to contact the ball at a level below the shoulders, using the forearms as the contact surface.

Free ball — A situation in which the attacking team is unsuccessful in mounting an attack and must either volley pass or forearm pass the ball over the net on the third contact.

Front set — A volley pass that is directed forward toward the attacker. In most instances the front set is directed to an attacker in position 4.

Frontcourt — The three positions on the court that are closest to the net – positions 2, 3, and 4.

Frontcourt player — Any player in position 2, 3, or 4 at the time of service.

Hit — See spike.

Hitter — See spiker.

Jump float — A jump serve in which the server takes an approach similar to that of a spike serve but contacts the ball similar to a float serve.

Jump serve — A serve in which the player jumps and contacts the ball similar to that of a float serve or a spike serve.

Jump set — A set executed while the setter is in the air.

Kill — An attack that terminates the rally in favour of the attacking side.

Let serve — A served ball that contacts the net and continues to the opponent's side of the court. Play continues as the rally is still considered to be alive.

GLOSSARY

Libero A backcourt specialist whose primary functions are to play backcourt defence and/or pass the serve. The libero substitution is considered a free substitution. Liberos wear a different coloured jersey than their teammates.

Lift An illegal ball contact in which the ball is in contact with the player for an extended length of time.

Line block A block in which the blockers attempt to prevent the attacker from directing the ball straight ahead to the near sideline of the court.

Line formation A three-person service reception formation in which the team receiving the serve align themselves in a formation, three across, parallel to the net.

Line spike A spike directed straight ahead to the near sideline of the defending team's court.

Linesperson Minor official positioned at a corner of the court, whose primary responsibility is to indicate whether the ball lands "in" or "out" of the court.

Match A contest consisting of a best three of five sets. A match consisting of a best two of three sets is also common.

Middle Usually the centre frontcourt player who plays in position 3.

Middle set A volley pass directed to an attacker in position 3.

Nonpenetrating setter A frontcourt player who is designated as the setter.

Offence Actions (techniques, tactics, and strategies) that are utilized with the purpose of making the ball contact the opponent's court.

Official An individual who is given responsibility to enforce the rules of the game.
See linesperson, referee, scorekeeper, umpire.

Opposite A player who is placed three rotational positions away (directly opposite) from the setter. For many elite teams, this player is a primary hitter when in the frontcourt and in the backcourt.

Out of bounds A ball is out of bounds when it contacts any object outside the playing area, including the antennae, or when it crosses the net above or outside the antennae into the opponent's court.

Overhand serve A serve in which the ball is contacted above the head in a manner similar to a "throwing" arm action.

Overhead pass See volley pass.

LEAD-UP GAMES AND DRILLS

Overlap
Incorrect rotational order of players at the time of service. A player is out of position in relation to at least one other player when the ball is contacted on the serve.

Overpass
A ball that is passed over the net to the opponent's side of the court.

Pass
General term used when contacting the ball below the shoulders with the forearms (forearm pass) or above the head with the hands (volley pass).

Penetrating setter
A backcourt player who is the designated setter. During a rally, this player moves to the net to set the ball, thus allowing a team to have three frontcourt attackers.

Pepper
A warm-up or ball-handling drill in which two players pass, set, and hit the ball back and forth.

Primary digger
The player in the best position to defend against an attacked ball.

Rally
The sequence of play from the time of service until the ball is whistled dead. The winner of the rally scores a point.

Rally-point scoring
A method of scoring in which a point is awarded after every rally to the team that won the rally. See side-out scoring.

Rebound angle
Angle of the contact surface of the body at the moment of ball contact, commonly referred to in forearm passing.

Referee
The official positioned above one end of the net who is responsible for the overall conduct of the game. The referee is often referred to as the first official.

Roll
Extended body technique similar to the sprawl except that after contacting the ball with either one or two arms, the momentum of the movement allows the player to roll over the opposite shoulder, returning the player to his or her feet.

Roll shot
An attack variation where the ball is contacted with the heel or palm of the hand with less than maximum force, imparting lots of topspin and directing it to an undefended area.

Rotational order
The sequential order of servers or placement of players on the court. Position 1 is the right backcourt player, position 2 is the right frontcourt player, position 3 is the middle frontcourt player, position 4 is the left frontcourt player, position 5 is the left backcourt player, and position 6 is the middle backcourt player.

Scorekeeper
A minor official positioned at the scorer's table, located behind the umpire and between the two team benches. The scorekeeper is responsible for ensuring that the score sheet is accurate.

GLOSSARY

Serve	The skill used to put the ball into play to begin a rally. The ball can be contacted by one arm only. The contact on the arm must be between the elbow and the fingertips.
Serve receive	The tactical skill of passing a serve.
Service	Aspects of the game that are associated with the technical skill of serving.
Service area	The zone behind the end line of the court in which the server must stand when serving the ball.
Service reception	Aspects of the game that are associated with the tactical skill of passing a serve.
Set	A pass that places the ball in a position above the net so that it can be attacked by a teammate. The volley pass is the primary technique used.
Set (game)	A series of rallies in which one team is successful in winning a minimum number of rallies. The winner of a rally scores a point. A set is usually played to 25 points, with a minimum 2-point advantage. The deciding set in a match is usually played to 15 points, with a minimum 2-point advantage. A set is commonly referred to as a game.
Setter	A player whose primary responsibility is to pass the ball to an attacker. The setter usually makes the second ball contact.
Shadow of the block	The area behind the block into which the opposing spikers cannot hit the ball hard.
Shaggers	Players who are not actively involved in the primary purpose of the drill, but whose responsibility is to retrieve balls and keep the activity area clear of wayward balls.
Shuffle step	A method of lateral movement in which the player's lead foot is extended in the direction of movement, and the trailing foot is then brought up beside the lead foot. This technique enables the player to shift while remaining square to the play without crossing the feet.
Side-out	Occurs when the team receiving the serve wins the rally and thus gains the right to serve next.
Side-out scoring	A method of scoring in which a point is awarded only when the serving team wins the rally. See rally-point scoring.
Sidearm serve	A serve in which the ball is contacted at shoulder height with the hitting arm fully extended and travelling parallel to the floor surface prior to contact.
Sideline	The boundary line running perpendicular to the net, from one end line to the other.

LEAD-UP GAMES AND DRILLS

Soft block — A blocking technique in which the blocker or blockers attempt to deflect the ball upward to slow down the speed of the opposition's attack.

Spike — A basic skill in which the player jumps into the air and hits the ball forcefully into the opponent's court. It is the primary method of attacking the ball.

Spike serve — A serve in which the player jumps and contacts the ball, as in spiking.

Spiker — A player who spikes the ball.

Spin serve — A serve in which the ball is contacted in such a manner that the ball rapidly rotates, causing the path of the ball to drop quickly or curve.

Sprawl — An extended body technique in which the player extends for the ball near the floor, contacting the ball with one or two arms. The player slides along the floor forward on the stomach or sideways by turning onto one side of the body.

Substitution — The replacement of an active player on the court by another player.

Support digger — A player who is not in the primary line of attack but can assist in defending an attack in a situation where the primary digger does not control the ball.

Tip — An attack variation in which the ball is placed or redirected with the fingers of one hand.

Topspin — The resulting movement of the ball when spin is imparted in the vertical plane in a forward direction, usually from striking the ball and following through by snapping the wrist. The trajectory of a ball with topspin will drop faster than a ball with little or no spin.

Turn and run — A method of movement in which the player turns to face the direction of movement, runs forward to reach the point at which the play is to be made, then plants the inside foot and pivots to face the play.

Umpire — The official positioned on the floor opposite to and facing the referee. The umpire is responsible for substitutions, time-outs, and general assistance of the referee (first official). The umpire is often referred to as the second official.

Underhand serve — A serve in which the ball is contacted below the waist with a forward and upward arm swing.

Unforced error — An error committed by a player that is unrelated to the opponent's play. It is commonly referred to as an unearned point. Touching the net, stepping over the centre line, and serving into the net are examples of unforced errors.

GLOSSARY

Volley pass A ball-handling skill that a player uses to contact the ball above the head, where both hands simultaneously contact the ball.

W formation A five-person service reception formation in which the team receiving the serve align themselves in a formation that resembles a "W."

LEAD-UP GAMES AND DRILLS

Notes

Notes

LEAD-UP GAMES AND DRILLS

Notes